Lord and Lady Macbeth

Full of Scorpions Is My Mind

a novel
by
John Passfield

Rock's Mills Press
Oakville, Ontario
2019

Published by
Rock's Mills Press
www.rocksmillspress.com

ISBN-13: 978-1-77244-169-7

Cover Design: Craig Passfield.

Author's Website: www.johnpassfield.ca

Chapter 1

Macbeth 1

Riding through the fog. As thick as witches' brew. The rain falls like a curtain. Our horses rear and plunge. *So fowl and fair a day I have not seen.* Unable to see the path. We could be riding in circles. We could be riding towards a cliff. *How far is't called to Forres?* The horses' ears are flattened. Their senses are on alert. If the sun would shine, we would surely know our way. *A drum! A drum!* Thunderclaps as loud as to split the eardrums. Lightning flashes that set the fog aglow.

To be the eyes

A horse plodding along in a well-worn rut.
A warrior fatigued from a high-pitched battle.
Figures looming ahead in the fog and the rain.

which discern the way

"The people of Scotland are no different from the people of any other land."

through this enveloping fog.

What forces enhance and what forces diminish?
What forces open paths or seal them off?
What forces light candles or snuff them out?

That howling drum again. I can hear it through the thunder. For sure it is a drum. Rain pouring down like a curtain. Mist as thick as a wall. *We three meet.* Horses making their way along inside the ruts. My cousin, Duncan, was such a fool. Placing his trust in that traitor, Macdonwald. The last man I would have sent to parley with Norway. He should have sent Cawdor instead. *Bat-*

tle's lost and won. Strange sounds. A kind of chanting. Growing louder. Spent swimmers clinging indeed. Standing around the campfire. Babbling after the victory. Not an iota of military lore in that pack of fools. *Fair is fowl.* Pulled my men back to distort his lines. Never in any trouble at any time. Waited until his lines grew thin. Waited for my moment. *Hover through fog.* Never too soon. – Never too late. What those fools around the fire could never discern. Brought his head back on a pike. Carried the head myself – on a sharpened pole.

Sunlight sparkling on a loch on a Scottish morning.
Flowers dancing in the breeze on a sunny hillside.
People singing and humming hymns on their way to church.

Riding along the trail with Banquo! Each of us nursing our wounds and thinking of what has transpired! We pace the horses as we ride, on our way from the battle to the king! The rain comes down, the way grows soggy, the daylight fades! We are easy in the saddle; our day's worst work is done! We each expect to prosper from this day! I slow my horse as the mud begins to thicken! Eventually we slow right down to a walk!

"The kingdom has been saved."
"There are reports of a great victory by Macbeth."

This is the moment - one decisive battle - bleeding on the floor - two earthly stones - a mother and her children - in deepest consequence - a hawk circling attentively - poor and single business - drift off into the mists - the bread and the wine.

I, too, thought of us as one from the earliest of days. One heart, one mind, one ambition. Our meeting was the encounter of my life.

That walk in the meadow was the merging of our destinies. We agreed on all points, my love. We flowed as one strong current from that day.

You were the only person to whom I could say what I was thinking. I was relieved that I could express my yearnings to you. You never flinched when you peered inside my thoughts.

The carriage creaked to a stop.
The horses grew shy.
"Is it either a gnome or a toadstool," someone said.

What is this looming up in the mist? Three of them, it would seem. *What are these?* Could be more, just out of sight. A nod to Banquo to be alert. One hand on the reins. The other on the handle of my sword. Those who live through perilous times are those who are careful. Stragglers from the battlefield? Norwegians lost in the rain and the fog? Doubtful with that chanting and that drum. *What are these?* This could be interesting. Up to no good would be my prediction. Deliberately blocking the path. Our only way, in this rain and fog. We will have to go right through them or we will surely be lost. *So withered and so wild.* Banquo is slow with his sword. That could have been fatal. *Th'inhabitants o'the earth.* So you are ready now, Banquo, are you? We shall soon see what they have in mind. We will give them what they came for – and maybe more.

Returning from battle.
Meeting those witches.

The trail has disappeared! We are riding in a bog, Banquo and I! My horse is breathing heavily! The weight of the mud on his legs! His hooves are sinking down with every hour and every mile! Banquo's horse seem rested and frisky! My horse seem tired and slow! Sinking down in the mud and the water! Hard to see in the gathering dark! Banquo rides along beside me! Why does Banquo ride on top while I sink down?

A man with eyes as clear as glass.
A man who knows every price which must be paid.

Devoid of speculation - better to make it sure - understand her role - nature seems dead -trampling the seed - i have in head - a very close family - see not the wound - joined under the surface - unless you are a macbeth.

The attraction was like to like. The attraction was stone to stone. The attraction was fiery sword to fiery sword.

You were swift with the gavel of judgement. You were kind to your frail old parents. But you judged them as you would a market-horse.

More alike, we were, than even you could have known. What you thought was a stable kingdom was built on sand. The kingdom of Scotland was no more secure than your father's throne.

A person drew a circle on a piece of paper.
"Our son and we together," said the mother.
"Our son and we together," said the father.
One! Two! Three!

What is all this chanting? *Live you?* What is all this noise? At least the rain has ceased. Now the drum has gone silent too. Not a military drum – some other kind. *Are you aught?* These people look so strange. Their beards, their voices, their faces. Such strange and wild apparel. Like nothing I've seen before. *Man may question.* Eyes, all three,that look beyond one's eyes. Seeking something deep inside the skull. *Seem to understand.* Holding my grip a little tighter on my sword. What folklore have I heard? An old fellow at the castle when I was a boy. What did he say about witches and faeries? *Her choppy finger.* Creatures of an elder world. *Skinny lips.* Did he say that they could speak true? Or were they like those ancient oracles? Dealing in truths or dissembling lies? *Should be women.* How would one test the worth of their sayings? *Beards forbid.* Should one act on what such a one says? *To interpret.* He'd whittle a flute and talk by the fire for hours. Can't remember now what the old fellow had to say.

Dead bodies littering a wet and muddy battlefield.
Voices calling a name from deep in the fog.
A question of who shall wear the crown.

Be lion-mettled, proud; and take no care who chafes, who frets, or where conspirers are: Macbeth shall never vanquish'd be until great Birnam Wood to high Dunsinane Hill shall come against him. Seek to know no more. Show! Show! Show! Show his eyes, and grieve his heart; come like shadows, so depart!

Armourers hammering swords in a smithy.
Warriors buckling on armour and mounting steeds.
Messengers racing with news of the latest broil.

Is loyalty sunshine or is it rain?
Is friendship armour or is it a sword?
Is honour a glass of wine or a witches' brew?

Just a boy when I heard those old stories. *Speak if you can.* Can't remember the gist of it now. *What are you?* Yearning, I was, to tilt with swords and lances. Thought old tales were only for old wives and young girls. *All hail Macbeth!* Should I test their corporeality with my sword? *Hail to thee!* What do you have to say about Duncan? *Thane of Glamis!* What of the stripling, young Malcolm? *All hail Macbeth!* Have you news, too, of the youngest one, Donalbain? *Hail to thee!* What are Duncan's plans for succession? *Thane of Cawdor!* Will he allow the thanes to vote? *All hail Macbeth!* Do you know what the thanes are thinking? *Hail to thee!* Has this battle made the name of the future king? *That shalt be king hereafter!* Who could possibly know the future of present things?

Meeting Duncan.
Riding home.

Up to my knees! Up to my haunches! Up to the reins! How can my horse keep his head above the bog? How can he move in such muck and such slime? The mud and the water threaten to overwhelm me! Banquo rides on top, oblivious of my plight! The day grows dark; the slime grows thicker! Up to my chest and soon my chin! Gradually, I feel myself sinking down!

A man who is at home in mud and blood.
A man who lives within the length of a sword.

An absolute trust - face current realities - telling me a story - constantly washing her hands - make myself the person - a spy in every castle - thrusting a pike - your eyes on my back - their welcome prediction - another place for me.

Feeble and tired was the old king, Malcolme. Unmanly and esthetic my cousin, Duncan. Scotland needed a ferocious warrior to face her foes.

I winced as these two feeble ones bowed down to foreign diplomats. Simpering as they showed negotiators through Scotland's halls. Bartering a fragile peace by offering stones from our castle walls.

I thought of myself as their future replacement. Every moment was put in service to what was to be. I trained long and hard to be ready when that time came.

A flower grew on a hillside.
Gentle breeze, white clouds, soothing rain.

So Banquo has ambitions too. *Things that do sound so fair.* Valorous in the battle – give him that. *Seeds of time.* Our names are linked in the Norwegian rout. *Which seeds will grow.* Granted, he had his moments. A courageous and worthy captain, it must be said. *Hail!* But surely his exploits cannot be ranked in the chronicle with mine. *Hail!* I it was who unseamed Macdonwald. *Hail!* I who beat the Norwegians back. *Lesser than Macbeth, and greater.* Those whom Banquo swept from the flank were lesser men. *Not so happy as Macbeth, yet happier.* You seem to know so much, so tell me, pray. *Thou shalt get kings, though thou be none.* What are those who have the lead of us telling the king? *Honest trifles.* So what will you do now, Banquo? *Deepest consequence.* Sit easy in the saddle, or brood all the way home?

A girl churning butter beside a castle creamery.
A group of weavers telling a story in tapestry.
A gleaner filling a basket amid the sheaves.

What have I heard? What have I heard? Old foot-soldiers, camp followers! Around the campfires, late at night! Howl of the wolves, cry of the crickets, light of the moon! Whispering of what they have seen and heard to unsettle callow recruits! Old, lame, poor, lean, deformed! Showing melancholy in their faces! Horrifying to all that discover them! Able to raise some men high and bring others low! Why, what have I to do with campfire tales?

"Macbeth has engineered a great victory over all our enemies."
"There is no force which can defeat the great Macbeth."

My first day of sunlight - the yellow leaf - a starving rat - if i turn back - thoughts have consequences - the stench of the battlefield - to practice your craft - scorpions cannot swim - what i mean as friendship - a little way into the cave.

I am not the kind – as you know, my love – to talk about our marriage. What is mine, I lock away like royal jewels. Once secure, there need be no thought beyond a smile.

I have always leaned towards action. Curb the tongue and draw the sword. Can we agree that almost every word has been said?

Better to talk about what we have learned. We have been through a lot together. We must glean whatever is possible from this stricken field.

An elderly person sat in the forest beneath a tree.
A spindle and some scissors were near at hand.

Bowing down to Duncan once again. How many times have I had to bend the knee? *Two truths are told.* Impossible to forget that I knew you long before you were fitted, my liege, for these kingly robes. *The imperial theme.* Now that the battles are over, you find it safe to pay a visit to the battlefield. *Supernatural soliciting.* Praising the troops that you failed to lead. *Commencing in a truth.* Dispensing booty you haven't earned. Bidding greater men than you come kiss your ring. *Knock at my ribs.* Not at the battle, royal sir? Afraid that your horse would have found the first pothole and tossed you off? *Whose horrid image.* You were the poorest of all the jousters. *Whose murder yet.* Always the one to claim that your sword was far too heavy for you to wield. *Smothered in surmise.* You are the fool who tried to negotiate for peace. Your weakness led the Norwegians to breach our realm. *Nothing is but what is not.* I blame you, my cousin Duncan, that Macdonwald threw in with the other side.

Wisdom comes in
with the tide
and goes out again.

A host barring the door against intruders.
The heads of traitors raised on poles.
A scorpion burrowing into a skull.

Wisdom bubbles up
from the earth
and disappears.

"Scorpions are one of the oldest known species on the face of the earth."

It is a rare and exotic flower
which is poisonous
when picked.

Of what significance is a crown?
In what way is everyone a subject?
In what way is everyone a king?

Two shocks have set me reeling. That Cawdor would turn his coat, who would have thought? *The mind's construction.* As you, my foolish cousin, Duncan, were fooled by him, so too, I admit, was I. That is the only point on which I have been equally foolish as you. *That is a step.* But to pick this young whelp, Malcolm. More shocking than Cawdor's defection by far. The poorest decision you could have possibly made as king. *Stars hide your fires.* All the worst of his father's traits. Wolves both outside and inside the tent will enliven his reign. *My black and deep desires.* Felt me breathing down your neck, did you? Have I made myself too apparent? Or have I simply been too kingly? – Too unlike you? *In my way it lies.* I was willing to wait, my cousin. I was willing to wait, my king. Now I find myself waiting for that which will never come.

Chapter 2

Lady Macbeth 1

We do not need witches – my dearest thane – to spur us on to greatness. *The day of success.* For us there need be no mystery as to their origins or their purposes. *More than mortal knowledge.* The only relevant purpose is the purpose which we shall assign to their welcome prediction. *Rapt in the wonder of it.* There is nothing in what they say that could not have been known or guessed at. *Weird sisters saluted me.* That you are Glamis is your right by birth and the sadness of your father's passing. That you are Cawdor is common knowledge by the rumours of Cawdor's treachery and the campfire surmises of the battlefield. *The coming of time.* That you shall be king is as right as the sunshine that follows the rain. *What greatness is promised thee.* You are Macbeth. You are Macbeth. You are Macbeth. Thou shalt be king. Thou shalt be king. Thou shalt be king.

To be the spur

A woman making a prediction.
A wine glass shared by two people.
An eagle tugging at its tether.

which provokes the leap

"The people of Scotland are no different from the people of any other land.

They want a roof above their heads, to keep them dry when the rain comes down."

to the lead in the chase.

Why put pennies in the poor-box?

Why send prayers up to the clouds?
Can the future be bent and shaped like iron in the forge?

You are so right to hasten to inform me of your thoughts. *Lay it to thy heart.* Your metal warms and cools as you contemplate the actions which we have considered. We must catch this updraught and soar while it is ours. We are never closer than when you see the greatness that is in your heart. We are one when we face towards greatness. – We are two when we face the lesser way. You must believe what these witches have told you. Not because they are witches, but because it is going to come true. Your wife has told you time and time again. You have told yourself over and over from your earliest days. Your deeds in battle have made you the man of greatest stature in the kingdom. *My dearest partner of greatness.* Not the witches, but you – my love – will have the shaping of this game.

Banners fluttering in the breeze on a castle wall.
A man with a patch over one eye.
Cripples on the edge of town begging for pennies.

I am reading the letter once again! I have read it many times! It is a very important missive! My husband always tells me everything he knows! The letter is a milestone! Our greatness is now assured! I keep it with me all the time! I only read it when I am alone! It is between my love and I! We drink from the same shared glass! – It makes us one! But there is something which I cannot understand! Why, oh why, are my hands so stained with ink?

"The warriors will assemble at Macbeth's castle."
"The two Macbeths will host a victory feast."

The speck at the end - the mind's construction - the back of my skull - she must have known - an arrow in the eye - coloured threads weaving - mediates the measurement - bow down in deference - what i want it to be - brackish bitter and fowl.

From the moment that we met I thought of us as one. In those days, I never thought of us as two. We were as close as any two people could ever be.

I had an offer from a miserable little prince from a tiny corner of Scotland. The scion of a tiny little island, battered by foreign adventurers and waves. I begged my father to refuse consent, and he complied.

My sister threw herself away – a handsome prince from a rag-tag kingdom. She disappeared in one of the raids. If she is alive, she is probably a waif in a prison cell.

"We have lost our way in the forest.

The woods are dense and dark.
We are hoping you can tell us the way," someone said.

You have grown too close to Duncan. *The milk of human kindness.* Duncan has grown too far from you. You owe him nothing from your youth. You were always far superior at every game. *Catch the nearest way.* Every thane has praised your generalship. Every engagement has proven your worth. *Wouldst be great.* You must forget these scruples of loyalty to a man who should not be king. You should see yourself as clearly as I see you. *Art not without ambition.* You do not need a witch to tell you that you are a king. Duncan should kneel to you as you sit on the throne.

Reading the magic letter.
Thinking about my husband.

I should put away the letter! The guests will soon arrive! I have read it so many times! The ink on my hands is turning red! It is moving up my arms! My dress looks like the butcher-woman's smock! I am sure that it is blood! What else would look and smell like blood but blood itself? The letter is from my husband! It commingles my blood with his! We share a glass when we drink our wine and our lips become stained! None of the servants would dare to notice! What should I use to clean my hands? What would the guests all think if they were to see this blood?

A woman whose husband is her life.
A woman who would make a perfect mother.

No mercy in heaven - a perfect copy - the bloody business - legitimate blood - this night's great business - test my footing -- i shall rely on you - facts are few - figments of my mind - visible through his chest.

Our blood has had one heart since the day we met. Our heads have had one mind in all we have thought. Every action has been the result of our single desire.

As a child, I used to love to feed the swans. They mate for life, my mother said, as we tossed the crumbs. The two are joined under the surface, I thought to myself.

My mother and father were so relieved when I gave them the news. A son in law with such regal promise was welcome indeed. You have surpassed every superlative that I presented to them on that day.

A creature drew a circle in the mud.
"The three of us, together," she cackled.
The three creatures danced together.

One! Two! Three!

I feel a lacking in myself. I have failed to raise you, my husband, to the highest level. You married me because I believed in you. *Not play false.* I am afraid I have let you down. You have that in your essence which is crying out for release. You are a king without a crown and a purple robe. *My spirits in thine ear.* You are subject to a nest of starlings who have invaded your natural realm. You are an eagle who has been tethered to the ground. I am the one who can lift you over the impeding stile. *The valour of my tongue.* It is I alone who can give you what is already yours. I must open you up to the gift that is buried inside your deepest self. *Have thee crown'd withal.* I must introduce Macbeth to Macbeth the King.

An island battered by storms.
A butcher-woman with blood on her smock.
A room at the end of a long hall.

He will not be commanded: here's another, more potent than the first. Macbeth! Macbeth! Macbeth! Be bloody, bold, and resolute; laugh to scorn the power of man, for none of woman born shall harm Macbeth. Listen, but speak not to't.

A lady and her son trading quips.
Sunlight shining on the stones of Dunsinane castle.
A man and a boy stacking firewood.

In what way can two people be seen as one?
In what way must two people always be two?
In such a fusion do we cease to be ourselves?

A messenger, out of breath, runs into the room. *What is your tidings.* He stops and bows and then gathers his thoughts and speaks. *King comes here.* So the king comes here tonight. It has taken me by surprise. *Mad to say it.* All things work for our betterment it seems. *Our thane is coming.* It is good that my husband will first be here. There is much that we need to say. *Almost dead for breath.* We'll put Duncan at the end of the corridor in the hall near the secret door. *Give him tending.* We will put his sons – the two of them, Malcolm and Donalbain – in the second chamber. *He brings great news.* Another term for predictions is planning well.

Greeting my wonderful husband.
Convincing him to grasp the future now.

There is blood on both my hands! Duncan doesn't seem to notice! He is busy praising his host! Nor, it seems, does anyone else! How could they fail to notice? My hand proffered as a gesture of welcome! Blood dripping onto the stones! The blood has moved to the top of my arms! My sleeves are crimson! He continues praising my husband! He bows and kisses my hand! He raises his eyes and looks at me squarely! I cannot resist a squinting stare! How can this be happening? There is no blood on his face! No blood on his hand!

A woman whose hosting skills are legion.
A woman whose castle is snug and warm.

Concentration on task - surpassed every superlative - probe the backs - a welcome respite - the courts of compassion - wade no more - shuffling in the dark - not just what I see - up to my waist - sleeping on the floor.

That walk in the meadow was the day of all my days. The flowers were blooming on the hillside and the sun was bright. I could barely believe how much we said with very few words.

We both had royal blood in our veins. I was an undervalued princess. My lowly status was an accident of birth.

And you were not the first man of the second row. You were Macbeth – with all that entailed. An obligation to take the fort at the top of the hill.

A serpent coiled underneath a flower.
Invisible presence, lethal venom, forked tongue.

I must be me and I must be you. I must be the two of us for as long as I need to be. *The raven himself is hoarse.* We have been equal for all these years, but there is a lack in you that I must supply from my deepest, darkest reserves. *The fatal entrance of Duncan.* I know – my love – what you are. *Come to my woman's breasts.* I know what you wish to be. *Take my milk for gall.* You wish to be more of what leads you to greatness and less of what holds you back. *Murdering ministers.* We have – both of us – let people toss us the dregs of the day. *Nature's mischief.* When the deed is fully accomplished, we can resume our old roles again. *My keen knife.* You can be equal parts milk of kindness and a warrior, fierce and bold – a perfect balance in a king. *The wound it makes.* I can return to the balance which you have admired in me – a woman fierce for her husband, but a kitten's kindest friend. *Blanket of the dark.* One fierce foray beyond our bailiwick and then home to the kettle and the hearth. *Hold, Hold.* Our respite lies on the other side of the fence.

A one-legged soldier walking with a crutch.
A person doubting his friend of many years.
A man with a scar across his face from side to side.

My father and I, alone! I have found the one I shall marry, Father, with your permission of course! You must have seen him in the courtyard the day we arrived! The young man who rode the black charger! His name is Macbeth! I'm sure you have noticed him in the throne room, around the fire, and at the dance! He must have attended those parleys that you found so hard to bear! We went for a walk in a meadow. – There were others present, of course! He is sure to be the next king, Father! He outshines that feeble cousin of his, of that I am sure! He was the one in the splendid armour! You remember the demonstration? The one who wielded the heaviest sword! The one who cut the contenders down as with a scythe! Yes – that is the one! I know he will be the next king! He spoke of his dream to me! He has contempt for his cousin, Duncan, though he was circumspect of course! I agreed that he would make a perfect king! We are compatible to our depths, Father! Much of our understanding was reached without words! We have agreed on so many things! He will speak to you, Father, before we leave for home!

"Macbeth is being honoured as the warrior who saved the kingdom."
"Now King Duncan will mentor an era of gentle peace."

The fabric of my design - what is more natural - my single friend in the kingdom - thorns on the way ahead - all i shall need - know our own thoughts - thinking kind thoughts - planting thoughts in their minds - face the lesser way - condemned to live that wish.

I used to watch the women weave the tapestry. I used to picture you and me woven inside. You and me and our little broken boy.

You enchanted me more than any three witches. And I have no doubt that I enchanted you too. We needed no predictions to enlighten our way.

Now the tapestry sits on the loom. The threads dangle down. The weaving-women have all gone from the castle.

Why do you sit beneath this tree? I asked the old one.
I sit and spin my thread in the nights and in the days.

A blast of trumpets. A tramp of feet. Some muffled orders in the hall. *Great Glamis! Worthy Cawdor!* My thane! My Macbeth! My love and my life! *Greater than both.* We must speak about this business before it cools. *Transported me beyond.* We have worn this topic smooth – a familiar path. *The future in the instant.* We have time and opportunity to do what we always have wanted to do. *Comes here tonight.* We must be one – more now than ever. *Tomorrow.* What I lack you must supply; what you lack I must supply. *As he purposes.* We must be the best that is in us. Two weaknesses must make for a dauntless One. *Speak further.* Further talk will only lead to further delay.

Solomon sawed
a baby
in half.

A woman ambushed at a crossroads.
Two swans mating for life.
A game for which there are no rules.

No mother
in the courtroom
claimed the child.

"Scorpions have eight legs and are recognized by their pairs of grasping pedipalps and their narrow, segmented tails which end in a venomous stinger."

Knocking frantically
on the door
was Solomon's wife.

What is love if it comes with a dagger?
What is love if it comes with a poisoned chalice?
Is love the gift which comes with risks as well as rewards?

There are two elements fighting in your bosom, as you know. *Never shall sun.* Only when you are in battle are you one. *Your face, my thane.* Your face – when you are in court – shows every man who wishes to read them your innermost thoughts. *A book where men may read.* You are not the one to parley and flatter and bow. *Beguile the time.* You are a warrior and a warrior speaks with his sword. *Welcome in your eye.* You must take your sword in your hand and be the person you want to be. *The innocent flower.* I am the person who can help you to become your hoped-for self. *The serpent underneath.* I have a plan – I have a plan. *The night's great business.* It will give the witches legitimacy. *Solely sovereign sway.* Whatever the witches are, they have no plan. *Masterdom.* Together, my lord – together – we shall do for you what those witches cannot do.

Chapter 3

Macbeth 2

Standing on the parapet. *If it were done.* Listening to the music. *Trammel up the consequence.* It is my castle, yet Duncan calls the tune. *Be-all and the end-all.* I am the victorious captain. *Bank and shoal of time.* He is the reigning king. *Jump the life to come.* The order of this realm is upside down. *Still have judgement here.* If there were no Duncan – no Duncan at all – I would certainly be the king. *Bloody instructions.* If Duncan should suddenly cease – the new king would be me. *Plague the inventor.* If Sweno had stood within my sword-length, he would not now be sailing home. *Even-handed justice.* There is no heavenly protection of the life of a king. *The poison'd chalice.* About being the cause of Duncan's death, I have no compunctions. *Our own lips.* Two buckets in a well. – As I go up my enemy goes down.

To be the balance

A king sound asleep on a royal pillow.
A dagger hovering in front of a pair of eyes.
A mind brim-full of human kindness.

which accurately weighs

"The people of Scotland are no different from the people of any other land.
They want bread on the table to keep their stomachs from aching."

the matter at hand.

Why would a man seek himself in a woman?
Why would a woman seek herself in a man?
Would man and woman not be better off alone?

The servants scurry from the kitchen to the banquet room. *Here in double-trust.* For Duncan the succulent capon and the roasted lamb. *His kinsman.* I am the mule who delivers his bounty on market day. *His subject.* He has been like this from his youth. *Against the deed.* Never lifting a hand unless to put food in his mouth. *His host.* And diadems in his pocket and gold in his purse. *Bar the door.* He has been lavish with nothing but praise. *Bear the knife.* Many a time have I suffered an injury in his cause. *Faculties so meek.* Mud and blood to him are the soil he wipes from his hands after he drapes the conqueror's medal around my neck. *Plead like angels.* Duncan's footstool, though dressed in gilt, is still his footstool.

A hawk circling attentively in the sky.
Moonlight shining on the castle at Fife.
A girl carrying milk in a bucket.

Two angels strip off their nightshirts on a cloud! I hold my hands up as I want no trouble with either! "Which angel are you?" I ask the one but I get no answer! "Which angel are you?" I ask the other with no reply! Both angels motion for me to remove my nightgown! They seem determined, so I hasten to comply! If it's a wrestling match they want, a wrestling match they will get! I test my footing just to see what I can see! The cloud is light and springy! It is my first time on a cloud! Not as soft as I would have expected! Wouldn't expect it to hold our weight! Not the best kind of footing for tossing your adversary, perhaps, but there are other tricks I have learned along the way!

"All of Scotland's enemies have been defeated."
"Foreign invaders and domestic traitors have been put to rout."

Offer instead of coins - full of growing - heads on sharp poles - lashing a man - a lack in my love - wasn't a factor - one that saw him die - meeting myself - fall'n into the sere - some light comes in.

Don't do anything rash, my love. Don't do anything rash at all. I have a prediction up my sleeve which will clear the air.

I have been in battles where the blood was up to my ankles. I have been in battles where the mud was up to my knees. Every human affair is a tide which is bound to change.

I have been pleased at how you have beautified the castle. Those window boxes in the courtyard are a fine idea. The taste of Duncan – and his wife – was so plain and so dark.

"The way forward is the way forward.
The way back is the way back.

The way sideways is the way sideways.
The way round is the way round," the gnome said.

My wife has left the feast. *How now. What news?* Perhaps something is amiss. *Asked for me?* Surely my thoughts have been clearly read. *Know you not, he has?* I cannot force myself to look Duncan in the eye. *Proceed no further.* I cannot raise a glass to his health with my hand on the handle of my dagger. *Honour'd me of late.* I swore allegiance at his coronation. *Bought golden opinions.* I carried the train of his robe. *Their newest gloss.* I captained the guard which gave the royal salute. *Cast aside so soon.* I cannot drink his health while preparing to shed his blood.

Greeting my wife.
Listening to her plan.

The angel on the left comes towards me! I size him up and shift to my right and he goes over my outstretched leg and tumbles head-first into the cloud! He comes up with a grimmer stare than when he began! We wrestle like this for an hour – mostly me making the holds, and he slipping out as best he may! After an hour, he backs away, and the other angel moves in to take his place! I am surprised that I have grown stronger! My old moves have all come back! And what has worked so well on the first one is working fine! He has watched us for an hour and has seemingly learned not a thing! A simple feint in one direction and he is baffled and confused! It never occurs to him that I would dissemble in making my moves! Finally, after another hour or so, he joins the other angel in repine! So exhausted are they that they both lie down as still as two earthly stones! I would have thought that angels would put up a better fight!

A man who will always fight to right a wrong.
A man who mediates the measurement of his worth.

The stench of the corpses - what we overcome - what is best for scotland - fail to acknowledge - there are other tricks - which would it be - nothing in this room - tells us truths - forget these scruples - never the same.

I knew, from the day I was born, that I would be king. Old King Malcolme was reaching his terminus. Duncan's colours were trailing in the race.

I had no inclination to redeem my father's name. His name had rated no mention in the annals of time. I was concerned with shaping the future – not the past.

Every tournament I entered. Every hunting party I joined. I saw as a test of my qualities as a future king.

The clouds grew dark and the rain came down.
The cold winds blew the paper far away.
Over hill and dale and mountain.
One! Two! Three!

This is not the proper time. *Borne his faculties so meek.* Perhaps on a day when we are under attack again from invaders. *Clear in his great office.* I shall be called upon to lead and everyone in the kingdom will finally rebel at Duncan's ineptitude. *Plead like angels.* I could, perhaps, refuse to serve. *Damnation of his taking off.* I could say that the foolish strategy of giving Scotland away – jot by jot and tittle by tittle – is the way to invite more invaders to trouble our shores. *Naked new-born babe.* I could give an ultimatum. *Heaven's cherubim.* Either Duncan must be deposed or I shall not serve. *Sightless couriers of the air.* The immediate threat would be so dire that every thane in Scotland would be sure to side with me. *Horrid deed in every eye.* Duncan would be forced to resign the crown and I would go on to fight the foe and win another victory and save the realm. *Tears shall drown the wind.* Then Scotland would be herself again. *Proceed no further.* The warrior and the king would be one man.

An angel blowing a trumpet.
A rider tumbling over a horse.
A martlet building her nest in a cozy nook.

Come, high or low; thyself and office deftly show! He knows thy thought: hear his speech, but say thou nought. Macbeth! Macbeth! Macbeth! beware Macduff; beware the Thane of Fife. Dismiss me. enough.

Messages being sent by secret codes.
A man who has ambitions to be king.
Meetings in the woods where no lantern shines.

Can two people merge into one?
Can one mind do the thinking for two?
Has there ever been the perfect fusion of minds?

My love, you do not know me. *Was the hope drunk.* I say the time is just not right. *Green and pale.* The news is carried by riders throughout the kingdom. *Art thou afeard.* There are torchlight parades in my honour in every town. *Act and valour.* Let me take a tour of the countryside, meeting thanes and building support. *Live a coward.* It is not for lack of courage that I would postpone. *I dare not.* Let me plant the seed that Duncan was wrong about Cawdor. *What beast was't.* Let me explain that Duncan is bartering Scotland away. *Screw your courage.* Let us build a secret cabal which will undermine Duncan.

Sticking place. I see no possible way to murder a king in this castle. *We'll not fail.* It would be perceived that our hands are stained with Duncan's blood.

Thinking things over.
Deciding what to do.

I put my nightshirt on! I go over to the edge of the cloud, lean over and look down! Below I see Dunsinane Castle and all its surrounding buildings and adjacent grounds! Is this the side where I gained the top of the cloud? I see no ladder! I walk across the cloud! The two angels lie without moving and neither makes a sound! I finally find the ladder! I am careful, and get myself over, with my foot upon the rung! I seem to descend for hours! I very seldom look down! Only occasionally, when I wonder how long this will take! Finally, I get a sense of the bottom! Then, I put my foot on the ground! The ladder disappears as I wipe my brow! I retrieve the key from the bushes! I stride towards the gate in the castle wall!

A man for whom the cup of life is full.
A man who toasts the health of every man.

A normal man - test your logic - every bubble of blood - what kind of a man - slogged in the thick - strong enough for two - i am only myself - rearing and plunging - stepp'd in so far - a story about you.

Banquo, Macduff, Malcolm – Donalbain, Lennox, Ross. I could barely refrain from chuckling when I measured their royal potential. Not one atom in all their beings bore the stamp of the future crown.

One day, Banquo nicked me in the shoulder. At the joint where the armour meets the helm. He begged me to call a halt, but I refused and battled back and won the exchange.

Macduff acquired a new charger from a far-away bourne. He entered him in the lists against my old roan. I won by a whisker, retired my roan, and acquired a new mount.

My cousin, Duncan, was completely inept in the art of warfare. Banquo and Macduff were out of their depth when they trained with me. I was the natural leader of every youthful game.

The flower had an innocence which attracted passers-by.
Those who stooped to admire the flower were sure to die.

Where the location? *When Duncan is asleep.* Castle or forest? *Soundly invite him.* What be the weapons? *His two chamberlains.* Daggers or swords? *Wine and wassail.* What of his guards? *Warder of the brain.* How best to subdue them? *Limbeck only.* Is Banquo in or is Banquo out? *Swinish sleep.* Inform

Macduff in advance of our action? *As in a death.* A group of supporters or just we, ourselves? *You and I perform.* What of his sons, Malcolm and Donalbain? *The unguarded Duncan.* Leave them dead or leave them alive? *His spongy officers.* What if the thanes all want an election? *Shall bear the guilt.* What are the odds of avoiding suspicion? *Our great quell.* How can we silence the tongue of every drop of his blood?

A tinker mending a hole in a pot.
A servant polishing a breast-plate.
Reapers building sheaves in a field.

What exactly is a witch? A witch is an old woman who is a scavenger on a battlefield! She follows the camps and gleans from carnage what she may! Let us say she meets some of her fellows after a battle! They take valuables from the corpses and ease the wounded past their misery and share the purses! They have heard the soldiers talking! How went the battle; what has transpired; how some of the soldiers say they long for a stronger king! They meet two captains in the field! They have hopes of a generous reward! They have nothing to offer to either but falsified hopes! It is rumour turned into gossip turned into prediction! There is talk of a better king to lead the kingdom! You shall be the next and your sons shall be next after him! Welcome words to a tired and battered captain or two! A moment's indulgence – a cooling draught of a whimsical dream! Hold your hands out for the expected shower of gold!

"Peace has come down from the heavens to dwell among us."
"From God to king to nobles to every Scot."

Found no such comfort - tell the old stories - sitting unnoticed - pushing drifting corpses - silence for good - seek to hide themselves - the shifting sands - like a battlefield - it is a knell - nothing but more thoughts.

No, I don't despise you, love. You have done nothing to me that I haven't done to myself. Every creature we meet adds venom or milk to our veins.

You have been a seminal midwife. Taught me to walk – taught me to crawl – taught me to breathe. You encouraged me to thicken my carapace.

You are the one who believed my dreams. How could you know that my dreams were hollow? As hollow as the tree that falls on the house.

"And what is the purpose of the thread?" I asked the old one.
"The purpose of the thread is to represent life."

You have sharpened my sense of intrigue, my devious love. *Men children only.* Your words have lifted an enveloping fog. *Thy undaunted metal.* You have seen into the heart of the matter at once. *Nothing but males.* A better time will never come. *Not be receiv'd.* A better time could not be devised. *Mark'd with blood.* I am blind to palace ways, but your instinct for palace intrigue is a thing to behold. *Those sleepy two.* Together we make the perfect pair. *Their very daggers.* Yours the plan and mine the sword. *They have do-ne't?* Duncan will breathe his last within these castle walls.

A master
fell asleep
on the homeward journey.

A horse sinking slowly into a bog.
A diver touching the bottom of a void.
A king throwing his crown into a cauldron.

His horse
was preoccupied
by the burr beneath his saddle.

"Scorpions are born one by one after hatching and expelling the embryonic membrane and the brood is then carried on its mother's back."

Eventually
the master
lost his way.

If I share with you a thought have I been your mentor?
If I withhold from you a thought have I done you harm?
If we join forces can we keep our thoughts at bay?

This is the night that Duncan dies. *Dares receive it other.* It was the plan that I was lacking – not the nerve. *Griefs and clamour roar.* I have always been a soldier. *I am settled.* Always answered the call with my sword. *Each corporal agent.* I have never troubled my mind about conscience at all. *This terrible feat.* As Duncan has lived, so shall he die. *Mock the time.* He had Cawdor put to the death with no squeamish scruples to plague him. *Fairest show.* The thanes were misled by the choice of Duncan. *False face must hide.* He promised peace but Scotland has suffered continuous war. *False heart doth know.* Without my victory, Duncan's eyes would now stare from a pole.

Chapter 4

Lady Macbeth 2

Watching Duncan from the battlements. *Hath a pleasant seat.* He and his sycophants down below. *The air nimbly and sweetly.* Banquo, Macduff, Ross and all the rest. *This guest of summer.* So all of you are supporters of this young whelp, Malcolm, are you? *The temple-haunting martlet.* You have turned your backs on my husband. *Heaven's breath smells wooingly.* All of your heads would now be on poles if not for Macbeth. *Pendent bed and procreant cradle.* So our castle brings you pleasure? *Breed and haunt.* Do you not hear the raven bark himself hoarse? *The air is delicate.* I make my fatal entrance. *See, see, our honour'd hostess.* I shall be your final hostess. *Sometime is our trouble.* You have worn your welcome smooth. *We thank as love.* It will be my pleasure to send you on your way.

To be the plan

A girl feeding bread-crumbs to the swans.
A line of severed heads raised on poles.
A splendid tapestry hanging on a wall.

which escorts us safely

"The people of Scotland are no different from the people of any other land.
They want a log on the fire to fend off the damp and the bitter cold."

to the sunlit meadow.

When we think of someone are we planting thoughts in their minds?
When they think of us are they doing the same?
Do some thoughts wither away while others grow?

Rushing down the corridor. *All our service.* The servants scatter out of the way. *Poor and single business.* Where is your lord, at present? *Honours deep and broad.* Where could he possibly be? *The late dignities heap'd up.* Such a burden to bear alone. *Your servants ever.* Why would he leave at such a juncture? *Where's the thane of Cawdor?* Duncan is a stickler for protocol. *Cours'd him at the heels.* Surely, he senses a taint in the air. *To return your own.* We must never let suspicion raise its head. *Conduct me to mine host.* We must play our parts until the curtain falls.

Mutes who have had their tongues cut out.
A woman who urges her husband to steal the crown.
Husbands and sons who go off in the morning and don't come back.

Sunlight on the castle walls! Stains of blood on the battlements! The creaking of the drawbridge chains! The raising of the portcullis! My first day of sunlight in a month! I pull aside my smock and draw my babe towards my breast! He attaches his boneless gums and begins to suck! The milk of life; the welcome sun; the freshest air! I am looking down at the activity in the courtyard!

"Scotland is now at peace."
"Thank God there is an end to these terrible wars."

Those which we choose - what i wanted to be - soaked in blood - a lucid defence - weighs upon the heart - yet-unborn thousands - shaping the future - that is a step - look for their places - what care i.

Sometimes I think that my blood flows in me and mine in you. Whose heart pumps the blood is never in question. Those times when we are closest are the times when common blood flows in our veins.

At other times, I wonder. At other times – confusion, disarray. Blood battering its head against closed doors.

At odds. Separate, alone, silently brooding. Thin as water, thick as mud, yours and mine.

"This is pretty plain to tell," someone said.
"You are no more help than a toadstool.
We were hoping that you would tell us what to do."

Confronting my lion in his liar. *Asked for me?* He is lodged in a window-seat above the courtyard. *Know you not he has?* Is this a time for leisure? For taking pleasure from a book? *Proceed no further.* To put one's feet up on the fender and brood by the fire? *Honoured me of late.* You must force yourself to be merry. *Bought golden opinions.* The castle is filled with triumphant revellers. *In their newest gloss.* We must foster a holiday mood. *Not cast aside.* They rejoice in your success and so must you.

Wanting the best for my husband.
Dismissing his minor concerns.

I am standing on the battlements! My babe is giving suck! I look down at the opened gates and the raised portcullis! The entourage of the conqueror riding through! A great commotion in the courtyard! Some are weeping; some are smiling! Many bow down in deference and offer spoils! The conqueror is reining in his prancing charger! Sunlight on his breastplate! One hand on the reins and one hand on his sword!

A woman who loves kittens and children.
A woman who is kind to the old and the ill.

A lady explaining - heard no more - the recipient's blood - what it's worth - as if nothing had happened - just to be sure - do anything rash - attending my own funeral - a circle in the mud - purpose of a banquet.

The old king, Malcolme, was inhospitable. His negotiations with my father were brutal in the extreme. He made it clear that my father was his footstool.

It was Duncan, the old king's grandson, who made welcome for my father. A sumptuous feast from Duncan – a beggar-bowl from the king. Duncan was younger then, though he came to resemble my father before he died.

Duncan's wife was feeble and helpless. She sat by the fire and sniffled most of the time. I could see that she lacked the attributes of a queen.

The creature snatched the paper out of the mud.
She held it out for the other two creatures to see.
"There are circles inside circles inside circles!"
One! Two! Three!

I see a lack in my love which makes me all the more his partner. *Was the hope drunk.* When is a warrior not a warrior? *You dress'd' yourself.* When is a battlefield not a place for carnage and pain? *Slept since.* What is there in us that will not respond when the trumpet blows? *Wakes it now.* We have talked about the kingship from the day we met. *Green and pale.* From that day we have known that someday my love would be king. *Art thou afeard.* Our best times have been when we sensed that the throne was the closest. *Art in desire.* Our worst times have been when the throne seemed far away. *The ornament of life.* There is only one meal to be eaten at the royal table. *Poor cat I'the adage?*

You must push your cousin from the stool and take his place.

A man and a woman walking in a meadow.
A princess languishing in a cell.
A dagger striking as deep as to the heart.

Say, if thou'dst rather hear it from our mouths, or from our masters? Pour in sow's blood, that hath eaten her nine farrow; grease that's sweaten from the murderer's gibbet throw into the flame.

Two grooms standing guard outside a door.
A ship sailing along a ragged coast.
An owl swooping down on a mouse.

Are people actually people or are they an idea in our minds?
Do these ideas surge on the beach and then withdraw?
Do they swamp us at times or leave us high and dry?

It is I who must act the lion for the good of the pride. *I have given suck.* I can only do this once. *Love the babe.* I only need to do this once. *Milks me.* I will make myself the person that we both need to be. *Smiling in my face.* Neither me and neither my lord. *Pluck'd my nipple.* But a new child born of both in the need of this night. *Boneless gums.* Gone in the morning when other selves will be required. *Dash'd' the brains out.* I will temper my husband's steel. *Had I so sworn.* I will be the sails on his ship. *You have done to this.* I will be the guide who points him out the way.

Considering all possible details.
Explaining the perfect plan.

I look down at the sunlit courtyard! I concentrate on the commotion far below! The conqueror dismounts and receives his due! My breath moves in and out! I almost swoon and catch at the castle wall! I am clutching at my babe! He is nursing at my breast! I purse my lips and clench my teeth! I lean over the parapet. My babe is sucking at my milk! I pluck my nipple from his boneless gums and dash the brains out!

A woman who makes friends easily.
A woman who puts her guests at ease.

Many fine days - the gift that is buried - troubles of the brain - shackled to a wall - think things through - horses lying wounded - flush the smaller birds - the taking of charge - bind us further - soft seat on the sidelines.

So I became a lady of the court. The Lady Banquo, The Lady Macduff, The Lady Lennox, The Lady Ross. I felt uneasy when the great ladies gathered in their splendid halls.

My mother was ambushed at the crossroads. Trampled down like a hollow reed. Treated like a maid at the castle door.

I knew a girl once – who was found at the bottom of a well. No one knew whether she jumped or whether she fell. It was not her task to fetch water in any case.

The flower tried to will itself to wither and to die.
It willed itself to fester and stink like weeds.

The plan is so simple it is as if it were made in heaven. *When Duncan is asleep.* I have planned it since I read my lordship's letter. *Will I with wine and wassail.* When I watched the ladies weaving. *Their drenched natures lie.* When I watched the butchers carve. *What cannot you and I.* When I raised the ladle and sipped at the cook's hot stew. *Perform upon the unguarded Duncan.* When I watched as Duncan dismounted his horse in the courtyard. *Put upon his spongy officers.* When I counted the number of diamonds he wore in his crown. *Who shall bear the guilt.* When he kissed my hand as I measured his neck for the knife.

Agents offering gold for information.
A man who leaves his wife and children behind.
People reporting a neighbour's talk to the king

Mother? I have some excellent news! The days of our humiliation are soon to be memories! My husband is going to be king! No more worrying about our fate now that old Malcombe is gone! Neither one of us trusts that shallow Duncan! But he will no longer be in our way! You remember, I am sure, how difficult things were for you! Sending father on each of those parleys! I felt for you as you waited for him to come home! Fears of it all being swept away! At the mercy of the selfish and the proud! Clinging to power at the whim of the one who wields the sword! To see our father and our husband so diminished! A little more tattered each time – a little more worn away! Let us ask the cook for some aprons! The flowers are blooming in the field! Let us go out and pick the flowers for the table today! My husband shall be king! His hand shall be on the tiller! I have no doubt that we two will succeed! We shall never be swept away by the wind and the tide!

"In every village of the kingdom people are rejoicing."
"Now they can sleep peacefully in their beds."

Thirsts after blood - tempted to tamper with fate - deficient in expertise

- lived long enough - keep such cold command - innocence is crime - brutal in the extreme - forced the gates - bring stability to the realm - need a moment of peace.

Birth is the miracle of all the miracles there might be. It is the way by which two people become one person. It is the way by which two people become three.

Our little boy would have been splendid as a prince of the realm. We could have had a little robe fashioned to fit him – and a little crown. We could have – the three of us – walked the red carpet during affairs of state.

Why are some women blessed with children while some are not? Do your three weird sisters – do you think, in such weighty matters – have any say? I have sometimes wondered what kind of prediction – if I could have chosen the topic – your three weird prognosticators might have made concerning me.

"And why do you cut the thread?" I asked the old one.
"Each length of thread is the length of a person's life."

Who could possibly detect a flaw in such a plan? *Men children only.* My love has waded through blood and carnage on the battlefield. *Thy undaunted metal.* He has razed castles to rubble that seemed, at first glance, impregnable. *Nothing but males.* He sees no drawback in the exercise. *Not be receiv'd.* Duncan will fall like a deadened tree. *Mark'd with blood.* The tallest fir tree in the forest will soon be king. *Of his own chamber.* At times my love is not my love. *Used their very daggers.* He is some other one whom I have failed to know. His face is Macbeth but his mind is not of my mind. He is lost in a mist or a fog. *They have done't.* So I meet him on the pathway. I make myself a fourth sister. I cast my spell and his better self appears.

I will build
the roof first,
thought the carpenter.

Boots trampling a woman like brittle weeds.
A baby sucking milk with boneless gums.
A warrior in command of a prancing steed.

It will shed the rain
when I build
the walls.

"Young scorpions cannot survive without the mother, since they depend on her for protection."

The foundation, too,
I can leave
for a rainy day.

Do we plant and cultivate people?
Crush their seeds or rip their seedlings out of the soil?
Do we clip and prune their beings as gardeners do?

I hold my lord and sooth him. *Dares receive it other.* I rub his temples as I often have done. *Make our griefs and clamour roar.* The blood of my fingers bringing warmth to the blood of our souls. *Terrible feat.* The secret, my love, will be that we will act as one single being. *Mock the time.* Two people with one single mind. One person with a double mind. *Fairest show.* Your thoughts will be my thoughts – My thoughts will be your thoughts. *False face must hide.* My strengths will be your strengths. *False heart doth know.* And our weaknesses – yours and mine – will fade away.

Chapter 5

Macbeth 3

Banquo and Fleance lurking like ghosts. *Who's there?* Whispering in the shadows with only a torch. *A friend.* Oh, Banquo you have dragged me into the mire. *To you they have showed some truth.* Without you – and this weasel, Fleance – I would have custodianship of the kingdom for all eternity. *Cleave to my consent.* I should have despatched you as the weird sisters pronounced your name. *It shall make honour.* If Fleance had been there, I could have bagged a brace of two. *My bosom franchised.* These witches are mortal, Banquo, mortal. I out-think them at every turn. *Allegiance clear.* You shall have much time in heaven to regret your decisions while here on earth. *I shall be counsell'd.* You have aligned yourself with the past – and not with me. *Good repose the while.* You shall never look down on your progeny wearing the crown.

To be the dagger

A single candle burning in a chamber.
A father teaching his son to hunt like a falcon.
A group of warriors gathered in a castle.

which points the way

"The people of Scotland are no different from the people of any other land.
They want a piece of land that they can call their own."

to the heart of the kingdom.

How many forces are at work in nature?
How many forces seek to influence human kind?
How many forces seek control of a person's mind?

I move swiftly along the hall. *A dagger which I see.* All is as my lady has said. There is just enough light to see – not enough to be seen. Secret passageways lead to secret doors. *See thee still.* The grooms are well taken care of. Their daggers are laid out, ready to use. *Fatal vision.* My wife is like a tiger. All nerves and doubts and fears are held at bay. *A dagger of the mind.* No doubt there was laughter and gentle chiding as they quaffed their fatal rounds. All the charm of an adder – and the charm of the charmer as well. *A false creation.* Both daggers should be employed. – I shall take them both. *The heat oppressed brain.* I listen before I move. It is the chamber at the end of the hall, of that I am sure. *As palpable as this.* I see the door is ajar – of course – she said it would be. *Mine eyes are made the fools.* I must remember everything that she said to do. *I see thee still.* I must make short work of this chore. I must despatch him without a goodbye. He should never have sought the kingship. My troubles began at that time. Who would ever have thought that the thanes would vote for him? *On thy blade and dudgeon.* I push my shoulder against the door. A creaking noise – but barely heard. *Gouts of blood.* The single candle gives a dull glow. The sleeping Duncan lies like a duck on a platter of gold.

A rolled arras covered in dust in a storeroom.
A hatter fitting a plume to my lady's chapeau.
A boy with a cage of fine-plumed birds.

Assembling in the chapel! The chapel at Dunsinane! King Duncan and his sons, Malcolm and Donalbain! Myself and Lady Macbeth! Banquo, my fiercest captain in the wars! Macduff, Ross, Lennox and the others too! The armies spread out on the grasslands! A mass of soldiers assembling outside! The priest bids everyone welcome! King Duncan turns and motions everyone to sit down! A simple ceremony on the eve of our great battle! A simple ceremony of the giving of thanks to our Lord!

"They say that the preparations for King Duncan's sojourn are lavish."
"They say that Macbeth is very fulsome in his praise of the king."

You are wrong - shun the investiture - laughter and cheerful children - which the eye fears - common blood flows - their promise fails - no secret doorways - plead like angels - a very conciliatory pledge - bottom of my mind.

Remember the meadow we walked in that first time? Tomorrow – if the sun shines – we can try to locate it again. A trick of the landscape – I would say – has made it so hard to find.

There will be days when we will walk in apple orchards. Days when we'll feel the warmth of the sun on our backs. The three of us together – you and me and the boy.

As for those travelling players, I had them silenced. I won't sit and watch tyrants being displayed on a stage. I won't watch depictions of kings, or rebellions or strife.

"Oh there is certainly more," the gnome replied.
"There is more and more and more.
There is more, but that is all I have to tell."

Duncan's bosom rises and falls. The sleep of the foolish; the sleep of the simple; the sleep of the stableboy or the porter or the blacksmith's dog. *There's no such thing.* The candle gives adequate lighting for all I have to do. His silver hairs invite him to retire, this night, to the clouds. *It is the bloody business.* Oh Duncan, Duncan, Duncan. A fool for once and a fool for always. Never sleep with your throat exposed. *The one half-world.* Always hire the best of guards. Never take refuge in a house which is not your own. Make it your business to know all secret passageways. *Nature seems dead.* Make it your business to know all secret doors. Make it your business to know what all creatures are thinking. Dwell inside their minds as much as you dwell in your own. *Tarquin's ravishing strides.* Permanent sleep will become you, my shallow cousin. You are relieved from a duty which was never, ever your own. An amiable lad who missed his true calling. Better an armour-boy for a warrior than a failed and futile king. *Hear not my steps.* I raise the dagger into the air. I hold it above his head and relish the moment. The man who has stood between me and my grandest self. The man who stands between me and my rightful throne. *The very stones prate.* I plunge the dagger into his throat and it is done. No – better to make it sure. *Take the present horror.* I raise the second dagger up and bring it down.

Seeing an invisible dagger.
Moving towards Duncan's room.

The priest intones the words! A special prayer for those who have died! A special prayer for those who are wounded! A special prayer for those who are widowed or who have been orphaned! A special prayer for the God-given victory! A special prayer for the safe-keeping of Duncan, our anointed king! The priest goes on and on! I am harrowed by every word! The time will come to say Amen! I will have a hard time to say it, I know I will! My throat begins to tighten! My tongue is as dry as dust! I am a soldier not a speaker! I try to live my life without words! I find myself with both hands clutching my throat!

A man who never wears a mask.
A man whose heart is visible through his chest.

Hiding in a foxhole - hesitate to cross - only have one item - my shadow on the wall - signifying nothing - every human affair - daggers at their sides - my human footstool - broken a trust - your most vulnerable weaknesses.

Then the old king fell ill. It was assumed that he was so far gone that he would not be recovering this time. People gathered for the watch from far and wide.

It was agreed that old Malcolme's successor would be chosen by election. That was decreed as the wish of the dying king. Nothing was said, of course, as to who would vote for whom.

When the old king died, I was as peaceful as if I had been attending my own funeral. I was as content as the old man himself must have been at his laying-out. I greeted everyone at old Malcolme's wake as if I was already his replacement as their king.

The creature held the paper over the boiling cauldron.
"The three of them are ours now! – Father! Mother! Son!
See I drop them into the circle!"
One! Two! Three!

I stop by the second chamber. *The owl screams and the crickets cry.* What has made me stop in my tracks? *Who lies in the second chamber?* I have these daggers to deliver. *This is a sorry sight.* I must take them to my wife. *One did laugh in his sleep.* See, I have done the deed as we planned it. I have slit his regal throat. *They did say their prayers.* I feel the need to speak but I cannot speak. *One did cry god bless us.* These noises are getting louder. Do owls ever scream so loudly as these seem to do? *Amen the other.* Do crickets cry with so much anguish in the dead of the night? *I could not say amen.* I clutch the daggers closer and closer. I have promised them to my wife. *Seen me with these hangman's hands.* I sink to my knees, here in the hallway. I move my tongue but I cannot utter a single word.

Two people walking in a meadow.
A man taking himself by the throat.
A diamond in the depths of a cave.

Double, double toil and trouble; fire burn and cauldron bubble. Cool it with a baboon's blood, then the charm is firm and good. By the pricking of my thumbs, something wicked this way comes. Open, locks, whoever knocks! A deed without a name. Speak. Demand. We'll answer.

Soldiers keeping to themselves in the taverns.
A prince who flees the country to save himself.
A kingdom under the fist of a brutal savage.

Is the future a waiting city?

Is the future a city which we build?
Is the future a city which we destroy?

How to tell my love what I am thinking? How to know what she will say? *Consider it not so deeply.* How can I speak of air-drawn daggers? How can I speak of owls and crickets? *Stuck in my throat.* How can I speak of Tarquin and I and what we have done? *Must not be thought.* How to tell her that I will be worthy of the men-children that she will bring forth? *It will make us mad.* I tell my love of the second chamber. *Methought I heard a voice.* I demonstrate to her on my knees. *Does murder sleep.* I ask my love my questions. *Macbeth shall sleep no more.* Why did I pause at the second chamber? *I'll go no more.* Why did I get down on my knees? *Afraid to think.* Why did I listen to those voices? *What I have done.* Why did I open my mouth to answer? *Look on't again.* Why did my tongue cleave to my mouth when I wanted to pray?

Slitting Duncan's throat.
Trying to say Amen.

I am clutching at my throat! I am fighting against my own hands! I stumble against the pew! My wife is knocked aside! The others back away! These hands are at my own throat! I cannot shake them off! I cannot say the words that will ease their grip! The priest continues on! He seems not to have heard the commotion! The others all turn and listen! A simple ceremony of thanks! A simple prayer for our good king, Duncan! When it is time, they all intone, Amen!

A man who measures friendship as one weighs gold.
A man who rides with one hand on his sword.

Every seed that I had planted - interim having weigh'd - sprinkling of thorns - a test of my qualities - the people of scotland - harrowed by every word - work for our betterment - on with my story - the surprise at the end - fluttering in the dark.

Shortly before the election, four people came to see me. Banquo, Macduff, Lennox and Ross. They said that they had agreed that they would not be voting for me.

They sat at my table in the great hall at Dunsinane and gave me their thoughts. We must do what is best for Scotland, they said. Macbeth is the man of war, they said, while Duncan is the man of peace.

After they had their say, I said not a word in reply. When they left, there were four knives in my back. When the time came, I never bothered to vote.

The flower could only project its aura, not its essence.
The flower looked more innocent day by day.

I hold out the bloody daggers as my gift to my wife. *I'll go no more.* She takes the daggers from my hands. *Afraid to think what I have done.* Of course, I should have left them with the grooms. *Look on't again.* They are a gift which I should never have thought to deliver. *Infirm of purpose.* A gift which I should have left in their proper place. *The sleeping and the dead.* She leaves, and I am standing here all alone. *The eye of childhood.* This moment has taken me by the throat – I must choke to death or seize this moment by the throat in return. *Fears a painted devil.* I must not be the man who paused at the second chamber. – I must be the man you thought I was when you were a bride. *Gild the faces.* I must strip myself to the core and build myself up again. *Seem their guilt.* What is the diamond that I must snatch from the depths of this cave?

A castle courtyard bustling with activity.
Boys playing at warriors defending the realm.
Two people setting-out place-cards for a banquet.

I want a word or two with those witches! Not a mention, in their predictions, of my wife! Any talk of future greatness must speak of we two! We two are one and the three sisters should have known it! They should never have spoken of me and my future alone! What kind of shallow insight cannot penetrate the skin? Inhabit other's minds? – you have no inkling! My wife and I have infused ourselves, one into the other! We inhabit each other's skulls! We move inside each other's corporeality! Together, our minds make more than two! Each of you three is a body alone – condemned to work singly at your tasks! We are a force which can rise above nature! We have had insights – as a single being – that no witch could ever imagine! – or even conceive!

"Apparently Lady Macbeth always shines at these formal ceremonies."

"They say she is better at playing host than the shy Macbeth."

A knife in the back - facing what I had done - a congregation praying - the core of the man - protection from their sting - planning similar scenes - the checking of swords - the telling of purer truths - in my way it lies - not yet reached perfection.

I descended into a deep, dark pit. Venomous toads at the bottom of a well. Better for you, I said, that I make this journey alone.

I was living at the edge of a desolate landscape. Fishing a little at the banks of Acheron. Saving pennies for the fare to the other side.

Bloody puddles in the driving rain in the courtyards. Blood-stained rushes where the dogs sniff crumbs in the dining halls. Blood-stained hands when I reached for the bread and the wine.

"And how do you decide whose thread to cut?" I asked the old one.
"Oh, I never know whose thread I choose to cut," the old one said.
"Who owns each thread is for someone else to decide.
I often wonder whether the next thread will be mine."

My love returns without the daggers. I should have taken them back myself. If it were to do again, I would certainly do so. *Whence is that knocking.* Her smock is a little smudged. We will have to wash ourselves. *How is't with me.* She had water fetched before she rang the bell. *Every noise appals me.* Who will carry the water away when we have had our bath? *What hands are here!* A knock like thunder assaults my ears. *They pluck out mine eyes.* It is the guests new-arrived at the gate. They are here to wake the king from his repose. *Great neptune's ocean.* They will see what they will see. They will know what they will know. *Wash this blood clean.* If only I could meet them. – Tell them what I have done and why. – Place everything on the table and have a frank talk among ourselves. *The multitudinous seas incarnadine.* Let every man speak freely, just for once. *The green one red.* I had rather give such a speech than hide my deeds.

The horse
grew frightened
and bolted.

An assembly of people mourning a fallen monarch.
A runaway horse with a boy on his back.
A man who chokes on the word Amen.

The little boy
hung on
for his life.

"When it is growing to maturity, the young scorpion's exoskeleton is soft, making the scorpion highly vulnerable to attack."

The parents
blamed each other
for the loss.

Is the future the rider's horse?

Is the future the horse's rider?
Is the future the speck at the end of the well-worn trail?

That dreadful knocking — loud and long. *Hands are of your colour.* The drunken porter is fast asleep. *Wear a heart so white.* We are counting on his tardiness as an aspect of our plan. *Retire we to our chamber.* Now we wash ourselves white as snow. *A little water clears us.* Now we take us to our beds. *How easy is it then.* Now we yawn and stretch when messengers come to the door. *Be not lost so poorly.* Then we assemble here in the courtyard in our new white linen nightgowns, and weep and wail at the loss of Scotland's soul. *T'were best not know myself.* I will go. I will go. Push me not. *Would thou could'st.* I will go and wash and put my nightgown on.

Chapter 6

Lady Macbeth 3

I am here in Duncan's room. Darkness envelops me. *Hath made them drunk.* A lone candle is guttering and fluttering in the dark. *Hath made me bold.* The hinges made a slight creaking sound as I opened the door. There is a faint light coming from the hallway. The guards are lying in the shadows. *Given me fire.* Duncan sleeps in the peace of dreams. If he had a greater grasp of kingship, he would not rest so easy. I am your hostess, Lady Macbeth. – Your time is up. *The fatal bellman.* I study the old fellow's face by the light of his candle. Why is he so alike to my father? I had forgotten that they are of an age. *The sterns't good night.* The daggers are ready to hand. I had thought to relieve my lord of his troubles but I cannot do what needs to be done. *Death and nature do contend.* I turn and tiptoe to the door. I leave it open for my husband. He will be able to see by the candle as he enters the room. The two grooms lie in a stupor and faintly snore.

To be the water

A hand reaching out to ring a bell.
Wolves wrangling over a piece of meat.
A maid showing ladies to their rooms.

which washes the night

"The people of Scotland are no different from the people of any other land.

They want the sun to come up each morning and go down at night."

clean of blood.

Why do people tell old stories?

What is the oldest story which can possibly be told?
Can one live through a story which has never, ever been heard?

I find my place and ring the bell. The servants have all been sent to their quarters. *Who's there?* Heed the bell, my lovely Tarquin, and it is done. Oh, what will he think when he sees his cousin? *What ho!* His childhood companion enjoying his dreams? He has known Duncan much longer than have I. *'Tis not done.* But then, my husband is a warrior. *The attempt and not the deed.* Surely he will have no unwelcome compunctions such as I have had. Surely the business at hand is worth more than gratitude or friendship or honour or any such trivial things.

Fathers and sons at one another's throats.
A country with her heart and tongue cut out.
Grim silence at every family table.

Tonight, I am going to kill my father! All the signs have said that this is the better course! I have even worked out a plan! Humiliation will be at an end! Crushing tribute and soul-wrenching treaties! Armour hanging in the armoury unused! Bits of our kingdom carved away at every parley! My father tossing meat to contemptuous wolves! My mother wretched and worn when playing hostess! All the great ladies eyeing our furnishings as we greet them in the hall! Making lists – as they speak of their friendship – to add to their spoils! And the contemptuous ladies' maids! – Looking down at my mother as she ushers them to their rooms! To be the tiny, tiny monarch of a diminutive kingdom! The moment-to-moment agonies of a minuscule king! Oh, my father, I bring you release! Better to die and sleep in peace for the very first time!

"King Duncan is being well entertained up at the castle."
"It is said that he lavishes praise on both the Macbeths."

Reach inside your chest - people bury treasure - spears and longbows - what i want to hear - hollowness in the pit - not the proper time - claimed the child - a taint in the air - strong enough for two - no unwelcome compunctions.

I threw myself wholeheartedly into my preparations for future greatness. I said not a word to those other wives of thanes. But, I must admit, I fantasized that the girl from the minuscule kingdom would soon be their queen.

We were invisible to all but ourselves. We were true to ourselves but not to our circumstances. We were the royal couple without the crowns and the robes.

Death, to me, would be to shrink as the years go by. Shrinking kingdom, shrinking husband, shrinking self. To disappear, yet still to be alive.

The king was very generous to his peasants.
With his entourage he went from town to town.

Oh, what are these noises in the hall? Who could be talking? *God bless us!* Why have I sent my lord alone? Perhaps we two should have ascended the stair together. *Amen!* I divided up the chores and perhaps should not have. Perhaps the two of us should have gone to the old man's room. My lord is in need of a partner of strength. He is not so strong on his own. *God bless us!* Noises again! And then again! Has Duncan waked and asked him what is the circumstance? Have the two boys come into the hall to see what is done? Have these grooms shaken awake and sprung to attention? *Macbeth shall sleep no more!* Oh, I should never have sent my lord to act alone.

Becoming another person.
Conducting a murder for two.

A little business outside my father's sleeping chamber! Cheerful chatter with the grooms! You have known my father long! How your children must have grown! I used to play with them in the orchard! We played the buttercup game! My eyes are drawn to their daggers! It will be short work I am sure! But keep to the task – don't fidget or falter! Best not give the game away! This is a quart of the king's very finest! Oh no, he insisted that everyone pledge him a toast! He is pleased with the latest parley! He has saved the kingdom again! Here's to the present and here's to the future! I myself don't often indulge, but this is such a special occasion! Bottoms up and I'll top up your flagons! Say hello to your son and your daughter! I would love to see them again! I remember those days in the orchard with fond recall!

A woman who takes an interest in other people's problems.
A woman who takes an interest in other people's lives.

Ask the old dog - should have known this - children who fear - nowhere to be found - sound and fury - betrays a sacred trust - the bars of a portcullis - mirror inside the mind - frankly he confess'd - custodianship of the kingdom.

I could not believe that you had brought away those daggers. How could you think that this was part of the plan? Standing there – covered in blood – with those daggers in your hands?

I was desperate to stop you talking. I felt that you were fitting us for the noose. It was all I could think of to try to save the day.

When Macduff asked, 'Wherefore did you so', he was showing himself in command. He was smearing you with blood, though your gown was clean. I had to squelch Macduff's bid to become the next king.

"We are as one," said the mouse to the frog.
"The same blood flows in me as in you."

My lord – at last, my lord. *I have done the deed.* What are these questions? Why question now? If the deed is done then the worst of the venture is over. All we have to do now is continue on with the plan. *Didst thou not hear a noise?* Surely this is much like a military operation. Do you worry about people praying on a battlefield? *Who lies in the second chamber?* Why, Malcolm and Donalbain – the kings's two sons. You were not to go into their room. *I had most need of a blessing.* Did you disturb the sons at all? What have they to do with this business? They must live to draw suspicion away from us. *Amen stuck in my throat.* Put them completely out of your mind and calm yourself down. My lord, think of Duncan as the traitor Macdonwald. Think of him as the usurping Norwegian king. *It will make us mad.* You are the man who slays his foes with no compunctions. The blood of Duncan's death will become the blood of our life.

A golden crown and purple robes.
Cheerful chatter and a toast to a king.
Spilt milk running among the cobblestones.

Gall of goat, and slips of yew silver'd in the moon's eclipse, nose of Turk and Tartar's lips, finger of birth-strangled babe ditch-deliver'd by a drab, make the gruel thick and slab: add thereto a tiger's chaudron, for the ingredients of our cauldron.

An old man sleeping peacefully in a bed.
A jeweller fashioning a diadem.
A cooper shaping barrel-staves with a drawknife.

Can stories tell themselves or must they be told?
Can stories alter themselves or have they no will?
Can a story cut out its tongue and refuse to tell?

What is all this talk about sleep? *Sleep no more!* Why would you say such things? *There are two lodged together.* Do you not remember how we both said that what would be sure to restore our sleep would be Duncan's demise? *The ravell'd sleeve of care.* Now that Duncan is safely dead. – Now that his sons are in disrepute. – Now that the thanes will be able to see that a warrior is needed. *Consider it not so deeply.* Now sleep will not only be yours, but sleep and peace will from now on envelop the Scottish realm. *Balm of hurt minds.* My lord, please calm yourself down. *Still it cried.* My lord, this is not to the purpose. *What do you mean?* I cannot believe that you are upset by a little blood.

Calming the fears of my husband.
Washing our hands of this blood.

It is my father who lies in this chamber! I have drugged the sleeping grooms! They were as supple as simple children! If only my father had been born with a little more nerve! To give away the kingdom, piece by piece, time after time! Feeding the throne into the fire to save the crown! I approach and raise the dagger above his head! Your hair is as white as snow! You have shrunk to the size of an infant! Care has worn you down to a nub! You will sleep well tonight, old fellow! Your daughter sends you to a better place! The meek and the mild have all things ready for those of your kind! You are short the scorpion's sting – the mousing-hawk's claws! Your pompous fellow kings will face the lion in terror now! My father breathes in and out! His chest rises and falls! Uneasy repose – troubled dreams – I can certainly tell! Mother says that he tosses and turns like this night after night after night! A surge of certainty of action floods my veins! Farewell, my sleeping father! I stand here with the dagger above your head!

A woman who revered her frail old parents.
A woman who was kind to the wife of the king.

Drinks the witches' brew - a hangman's noose - to look clear down - a fine idea - with honest trifles - tethered to the ground - the righteous arrow - the first to see this - you durst to it - any portion of the plan.

Duncan's wife. Her Majesty, the Queen. Her cold and draughty castle.
We were sitting by the fire. A blanket over her head. A runny nose.
"My husband is not a warrior," she said. She blew her nose with the royal handkerchief. "But everything he does is for Scotland's good."

"Steal a penny and the king cuts off an index finger,"
said the man with only one arm.

Think of water, my dear lord. Think of water rather than blood. *Unbend your noble strength.* A well of water – a moat of water – an ocean of waves. We will cleanse whatever is bothering you away. *So brainsickly of things.* But what of this? What have you here? What of these daggers! You should have left them in the hallway. – That was the plan. You are undermining the plan when you act this way. *This filthy witness.* Give me. Give me. Let go. You must release your grip my lord. *Infirm of purpose.* I assure you. – You need not leave this place. – I shall go.

Rumours about a meeting of thanes in England.
A host who turns and stabs his trusting guest.
People going for walks so they can talk.

A cold day in the castle! Huddling up to the fire! Cloistered with Duncan's wife! A woman embraced by death! A sickly, wheezing little biddy! A newcomer would mistake her for the maid! Thank you, your Majesty, for inviting me here to await the arrival of my husband! Each time he ventures out, I am left alone! I see your husband is a worrier! Much is hazarded on this push! I trust my husband – and of course, Banquo – will deliver the hoped-for rewards! Your husband shines in the parleys, my husband tells me! I assume young Malcolm will do so as well! And what of Donabain? – I wonder what he will become! My husband says that a kingdom is only strong if its warriors are equal to the task of keeping it safe and secure and free! He is always pleased to present his victories to his king! You do not look well, your Majesty! Press closer to the fire! Shall I call for an attendant? Mulled wine is good for the cold! The fates have smiled on you, your Majesty! My husband has always wanted sons! Are your sons with their father? I assume that neither boy has gone into the field!

"We can raise our children in peace."
"From now on our old folks will rest secure."

Signs of nobleness - the sleep of the stableboy - paid the cost - smiling in his rocking chair - alone on that barren heath - to grasp the future - an ear-splitting drum - disappears inside the helm - undermining the plan - i read the faces.

I had them take old Malcolme's tapestry down. Behind was a cold, stone, draughty wall. I tried to imagine the magnificent pageant – with a brilliant array of splendid colours – which was being designed as a chronicle of our reign.

The master-weaver was a martinet. He worked the weavers very hard. But he was a man who loved the lore of his trade.

"A good tapestry will last for centuries," he said. "A record of the deeds that were done in this time. The eyes of yet-unborn thousands will marvel at the events which will animate this wall."

Two scorpions met on the bank of a river.
"Will you carry me on your back?" asked one.

The grooms lie peacefully in the hall. *The sleeping and the dead.* I enter Duncan's room again. He is lying in the dark. Well, his death has gone well, at least. The candle throws my shadow on the wall. *The eye of childhood.*

I pause and move towards him. Yes Duncan – it is your hostess. This will only take a short while. Your face no longer resembles my father in sleep. *A sleeping devil.* A task of but a few moments. I bend over him and lave the daggers in his blood. *Guild the faces.* I pause and wipe my brow with my sleeve. Perspiration runs down my temple. I turn around and move towards the door. My husband and I have done too much thinking tonight. It is best not think at all. The door creaks on its hinges and I am gone.

A vagabond
stole
a treasure.

A mousing-hawk extending its claws.
A rolled tapestry covered in dust in a storeroom.
Two people sleeping peacefully with blood on their hands.

Curs'd Be He
Who Opens
Me First!

"Scorpions are nocturnal, finding shelter during the day in underground holes or the undersides of rocks, emerging at night to hunt and feed."

It is time
I had a partner
for my crimes.

If I tell a story about you do I own you?
If you tell a story about me am I your slave?
Does our story place its shackles on us both?

Returning to my husband in the courtyard. *Of your colour.* A dreadful knocking at the gate. *A heart so white.* Has the morning come so soon? *Retire we.* We must hurry on with our plan. *A little water clears us.* I ignore my husband's protests. *How easy it is then.* The deed is the deed – and the deed is done. *More knocking.* Spilt milk is a problem for dairy maids and cooks. *Your nightgown.* I hurry him from the courtyard. *Occasion call us.* We do not have time to talk like this. *Be not lost.* We must wash and put on our nightgowns. *To know my deed.* We must appear to be surprised by these events. *Not know myself.* Your thoughts are pertinent, my lord, but they are not timely. *Wake Duncan.* Plenty of time in the years ahead to consider these things.

Chapter 7

Macbeth 4

Macduff and Lennox chatting with the Porter. Here to wake Duncan are you? *Good morrow to you both.* We shall see how far you get. *Not yet.* Always talking of your children. You will have some stories to tell. He will resemble, perhaps, your father as he sleeps. *I'll bring you to him.* Off you go, this fine morn, to greet your sleeping sovereign. *The labour we delight in physics pain.* I have already said my farewell – a farewell that is much in tune with Duncan's progress. *This is the door.* Life is short– and sometimes shorter. Yes, the king goes forth today – for once and for all.

To be the knocking

A group of people gathered in a courtyard.
A creature digging hemlock in the dark.
A man sitting and staring at a tapestry.

at the door

"The people of Scotland are no different from the people of any other land.
They want the leaves to sprout in the spring and to fall in the autumn."

which brings good news.

Does nature notice what humans are busily doing?
Is nature influenced at all by human thought?
Does nature seek to influence human kind?

Well, Duncan, you shall be leaving soon. I shall carry you one last time. *He does; he did appoint so.* I have done you and your boy a favour.

Relieved you both of offices whose weight was beyond your scope. And you, Macduff – I know what you are thinking. Your eyes are telling their credulous story to your sleepy surmise. Duncan laced with silver blood. The gilded faces of the grooms. The daggers left so tellingly in their place. You are enlisting in this night's enterprise as our greatest ally. So sorry that I cannot thank you for your support. *T'was a rough night.* A little Macduff will clear us of this deed.

A king and queen riding through a market square.
Herbs and spices being sprinkled into a pot.
Men watching a hawk as it cruises the sky.

Approaching the courtyard in my nightshirt! Wondering whether to hide my hands! I scrubbed for a long hour but the blood would not be cleansed! Lennox looks askance and makes no comment! Maduff seems more concerned to be late for the king! I hold out my bloody hands and exchange a greeting with each of them! Neither seems to mind what he can see! Is the blood so soon invisible? Why did I wash my hands for so many hours? What is a little blood on my smock and on my hands? I should never have let it bother me! I would be holding the daggers now but my wife took them both away to take back to the king!

"There are plenty of rumours this morning up at the castle."
"People are crowding around the gates to find out what goes on."

The midst of this fantasy - sweet oblivious antidote - bereft at her funeral - the scorpion is blind - making a list - called upon to lead - plenty of rumours - what leave behind - huddling silently - shrinking self.

As for sleeping and dreams and such, my love, I almost never sleep. I storm through the all-night scullery and catch the night-watch napping. I have my horse saddled at midnight and go out for a ride.

I don't believe in deepest thoughts, my love. There are none. If the puddles on my path were not shallow, I could not go on.

And as for looking every man in the kingdom in the eye. And every woman and child too, I might add. When you are the king of all the kingdom, you need not try.

Every market day the king would appear among his people.
He gave each peasant a gift from a bulging sack.

Clattering on the staircase. *Confusion's masterpiece.* Stricken faces, gasps for breath. *Lamentings heard in the air.* Macduff is explaining what he has seen. *Most sacriligeous murder.* Taking the hook. Swallowing the bait. *What's the matter?* Macduff the honest messenger – acquitting me of my crime. *The lord's annointed temple.* Brave lass, your plan is working. The execution of a perfect campaign. The drinks, the daggers, the nightgowns. A truly brilliant plan. We shall hold hands as we walk along life's path. *Strange screams of death.* We shall greet Macduff at Scone before too long.

Acting surprised at the murder.
Lamenting Duncan's loss.

Why should I pretend to be what I am not? I am the king's despatcher! A warrior who has done a warrior's deed! I stood there after the battle with Macdonwald's blood on my armour! Everyone said that I had been brave and done the right thing! Now I stand here in my smock and show my bloody hands and arms for all to see! I have done this deed for Scotland! Duncan was drifting at the helm! Every parley was a diplomatic defeat! Scotland was slowly being engulfed by a hostile sea! Whose children will not be safer? Whose old parents will not sleep more soundly? I hold out these bloody hands – I exhibit this bloody smock – to prove that I am the man to take over the helm!

A man whose marriage is forged in the hottest fire.
A man who wife is the rock on which he stands.

Hard-pressed to say - rubbing the temples - an old wives' tale - hear the raven bark - the way forward - cool inside her armour - relieved from a duty - i think no thoughts - told by an idiot - behaves like a ghost.

That night marked the return of my boyhood fits. I rolled around in the rushes with the dogs. You held me in your arms and rubbed my temples.

I remember very little of Duncan's coronation. I attended, but can recall almost nothing at all. I was a man who had been hollowed out to the core.

I felt your eyes on my back as I knelt in fealty to Duncan. All my ambitions gasping for life in the mud and the blood. You had seen inside my dream and there was nothing there.

"We are as one," said the frog to the mouse.
"The same blood flows in me as in you."

Bursting into the chamber. *What is't you say?* Lennox examining the king. *The life?* Me, looking over my shoulder. Is Macduff still outside? A very calm demeanor at a time like this. More calm than brave Macduff was able to muster. *Dire combustion and confused events.* Dead for sure? Dead for sure? Of course he is. There can be no doubt. *Remembrance cannot parallel.* No shoddy workmanship here. My lady and myself, we have our pride. When we despatch, we despatch for good. There are no returns.

A man with dripping blood on his hands.
Shallow puddles on a pathway.
A man with his hands over his ears.

Double, double toil and trouble; fire burn and cauldron bubble. Scale of dragon, tooth of wolf, Witches' mummy, maw and gulf of the ravin'd salt-sea shark, root of hemlock digg'd i' the dark.

Heads on poles above the bridges along the rivers.
A king who fails to keep his nobles in line.
Soldiers on guard on castle walls.

Does destiny hunt with a net and a spear?
Does destiny hide when it sees us coming?
Does destiny sit and wait with its apron open wide?

Turning and shuffling out into the hall. Lennox playing his part so well. *Those of his chamber.* Well played, well played, well played. Pulling a cart with a ring in his nose. *Badged with blood.* Lennox moving along the hall. Myself staying behind. *Daggers unwiped.* Clutching the dagger in my hand. Raising it up and striking a blow. *Staring.* Kill Duncan will you? Kill the King and then lie here sleeping? *Distracted.* And you – you would shirk your office? Take a wee dram while at your post? Well, here's remembrance for your pains! *No man's life.* Remember the porter as you enter in at the gate!

Killing the sleeping grooms.
Explaining why I did so.

We are all political here! We can all face current realities! If your father is no longer king, you must bow to he who now is! Malcolm seems to take it manfully! He bows down and kisses my ring! He rises with not a spot of blood on his face! Donalbain seems cheerful enough! It is not he who would have been king! Now his brother will have more time for the hunting of game! Banquo, Macduff, Lennox, Ross! All seem to have settled down! The lion has roared his eminence! The owl has caught his mouse! The king is dead; we have a new king; now let us get on! No more raids on our women and children! Plowmen and shepherds will not be sniffing each idle wind! The sun has always risen. The cock will always crow. What is more natural than to accept what comes to be?

A man whose honour is the foundation on which he builds.
A man whose valour is the fuel which drives him on.

There is a force - yoked themselves together - rubbing the temples - no further plans - fear in the eyes - no known cure - spend a normal day - birth is the miracle - will be your moment - safe and secure and free.

The bonfires carried the news far and wide. Duncan had become the Scottish king. The man of war held in shackles by the man of peace.

How could they carry on with life as if nothing had happened? Banquo, Macduff, Malcolm? – Lennox, Ross? How could they see me as anything other than a ghost?

I walked and talked as a normal man. I wielded my sword in every friendly encounter with a vengeance which must have screamed. How could they fail to see the rage with which I boiled?

"Steal a loaf of bread and the king cuts off a hand at the wrist," said the man with only one arm.

Reporting to Macduff. Trying so hard to read his face. A glint of suspicion, it seems to me, has entered his eye. Saying all the things that Macduff expects to hear. *Who can be wise, amazed, temperate?* That Duncan was our king. *Outran the pauser, reason.* That Duncan's life has been taken. *Unmannerly breach'd with gore.* That this is a terrible thing. *Looked like a breach in nature.* That we all are horror-stricken. *Ruin's wasteful entrance.* That somehow we must carry on as best we may. *Colours of their trade.* All the while watching Macduff. Who, I wonder, is the real Macduff? All the while trying to read behind the eyes.

A dressmaker sorting yards of cloth.
Friends sipping wine beside a fire.
Singers and musicians bowing for their guests.

If only I had cut the three sisters down before they spoke of Banquo! If only I had slaughtered them before they were able to speak! If only I had been alone on that barren heath, no doubt the prediction would have been mine and mine alone! If only Fleance had been there with Banquo, I could have ended this agony on the instant, then and there! I had the future in both my hands and I let it go!

"Most of the rumours seem to centre on the health of the King."
"The castle gates are barred and no one gets in or gets out."

To influence human kind - fortify a church - blood aplenty - find good sleep tonight - with very few words - the twitch of a paw - my own hands clean - invisible presence - wherefore did you so - that walk in the meadow.

I withdrew from you the day that Duncan was crowned. I had failed you in the thing that mattered most. Every seed that I had planted had failed to grow.

A hollowness in the pit of my stomach. A raging fever in my brain. How could I look my wife – now – squarely in the eye?

I sat by the fire. I stared at old Malcolme's tapestry. I went for long rides in the fog and the rain.

"I cannot carry you," the other scorpion replied.
"I too am a scorpion and scorpions cannot swim."

Wherefore did you so? Wherefore did you so indeed. Do you dare to question me? Do you dare to question Macbeth, who shalt be king? The ladder is leaning against the wall. I have already begun the siege. Fall in behind if you wish to share the spoils. Do you challenge me for the kingship? Do you? Two scorpions meeting on a log across a divide? You shall find me ready enough. I have a partner – a partner of greatness. *Broke ope!* – Broke ope! It was I who broke it open! It was I who forced the gates! Duncan's servant or Duncan's successor – which would it be? Oh go home and play with your chickens! Close the gate when you get to Fife! Wherefore did you so? – Wherefore did you so? You dare to ask?

The clock sounded
in the
market square.

A man bowing down and kissing a ring.
A pair of eyes that read behind the eyes.
A man rolling around among the dogs.

An old man
covered
his ears.

"Some, but not all, scorpion species have male and female individuals."

If I were deaf
I would not have to think
about the passage of time.

Can a witch create a human?
Can a human create a witch?
Can witches and humans mate and produce a child?

Help me hence, ho! My lady slowly sinks to the floor. I am too amazed to move. Lennox comforts her while I stand here and stare. What is this fainting at one's post? While I am carrying out our plan. Is this a ruse to draw attention? *Look like the innocent flower.* Are my words not to the point? When we make a plan, my lady, we should both of us be firm in carrying it out. *Your face is as a book.* Are the others fooled or am I? I cannot think what you are doing, Lass. What is the purpose of this feint? *Look to the lady.* You have baffled me, my girl, but what of the others? I would like an explanation. We must talk before we make our future plans. You and I must speak the same language or hold our tongues.

Chapter 8

Lady Macbeth 4

This night has been a nightmare. We try to be ghosts as we move in our chamber. We have left our bloody clothes in the secret cell. We dare not touch any of the objects in our room. Perhaps the hardest part is over. The killing was much more difficult than I ever could have imagined. Now the discovery is the hurdle that we must face. Both nightgowns lie out ready. Not a spot on either one. My husband seems lost in a trance as he washes and washes and washes again. He has taken this much more troublingly than I thought he would do. Washing blood from the hands is easier than washing the mind.

To be the sun

Bloody clothing hanging on pegs on a bare, stone wall.
A person carrying another across a stream.
A travelling player acting in a play.

which brings good cheer

"The people of Scotland are no different from the people of any other land.
They want the ground to be ready for tilling and planting the seed."

to the waiting day.

Can an idea clutch a dagger?
Can an idea heft a sword?
Can an idea cleave a will to its mould?

Wiping some blood from off your elbow, my love. Washing the spots of blood from your feet. We were giggling as we were trying to wash in the dark. The blood is much more visible, here in the morning light. Remember to show yourself as a sleeper. Yawn and stretch as you come into the courtyard. You can play this part well, I am sure. You have stridden through blood on battlefields many a time. Remember why we have done this. This was for Scotland and Scotland alone. Duncan was not the king for this kingdom. Others have known that since he was crowned, but not said it aloud. Here, my love, before you go, let me wipe, once again, your fevered brow.

Carpenters hewing beams for battering rams.
A kingdom invaded by armies of savage adventurers.
An old woman tending a wound to her grandson's side.

I am wading across a stream! Fording a stream on the trail! I am carrying a heavy, heavy burden! I am carrying my husband on my back! The stones are slippery; the water runs fast; I place each foot carefully forward! At times I graze my foot against a stone! He is telling me a story about a scorpion! A scorpion who asks for a ride on another's back! At times the stones shift and the current tugs hard at my waterlogged skirts! My husband goes on with the story! He clings to me as I stumble, at times, and almost fall! I strain to see my feet in the muddy water! I dare not raise my eyes to look ahead!

"There are all kinds of rumours coming out of the castle."
"Rumours are plenty; facts are few."

That howling drum - rumours about a queen - all things set to rights - control the discourse - the grip of sleep - your empty throne - nothing is - refuse to serve - choose my footing carefully - designed to paralyse.

Which of the couples did you most admire? The couple Banquo, the couple Macduff, the couple Lennox, the couple Ross? You knew all these couples much longer than did I.

Of course, I never knew my mother and father when they were younger. During my childhood, I thought them alike in many ways. Whether they started out that way or grew together, I would be hard-pressed to say.

To be alone has always been my greatest fear. To not share my being with another is a fate that I dread. I am only myself if I am at one with my lord.

In the sack were golden crowns.
Every one a perfect copy of the crown on the king's own head.

Wiping the blood off one of my feet. Ruffling my nightgown so it looks as if I've had some sleep. I must be strong enough for two. What can I say that will bring him back to what he was? The brave captain who never flinches when faced with the enemy. The warrior who slices his opponents from the nave to the chaps. The feelings that he has for Duncan have been quite a surprise. He never spoke that way of Duncan when his cousin was alive. I nerved myself up to make him stronger. I couldn't have known what a draining task that would turn out to be. I try to bring out what I feel is the core of the man. I think of myself as him and of him as me. We are one in our heads and in our hearts. What will I do if he ever turns his face from me?

Yawning and purring and stretching.
Asking what is amiss.

My husband is wading across a stream! Fording a stream on the trail! He is carrying a heavy, heavy burden! He is carrying me on his back! The stones are slippery; the water runs fast; he places each foot carefully forward! At times he grazes his foot against a stone! I am telling him a story about a scorpion! A scorpion who asks for a ride on another's back! At times the stones shift and the current tugs hard at his heavy armour! I go on with my story! I cling to him as he stumbles, at times, and almost falls! He strains to see his feet in the muddy water! He dare not raise his eyes to look ahead!

A woman who is close with the other wives of the court.
A woman who is gentle in the management of her servants.

Chosen different threads - attempting to ford - withdrew from you - re-visits the scene - like the poor cat - time and the hour - the way back - hesitate to cross - must remain calm - played the buttercup game.

I did not see any reason to eliminate Banquo. If you had thought about it, you would have felt the same. 'Banquo's issue shalt be kings' – what could that mean?

I looked at the Banquo situation like this. You reign for a good many years and then our son succeeds his father. Then Banquo's issue – far beyond the natural life of Fleance, of course – comes into its own after an interminable irrelevancy of years.

I try to be logical – always logical. I think things through to the end. The witches never said that Fleance would be king.

The mouse and the frog yoked themselves together.
The same blood flowed in one as in the other.

Listening secretly to Macduff as he speaks in the courtyard. *Oh horror! Horror! Horror!* Where is my husband in all of this? *Tongue nor heart cannot conceive.* Do I faintly hear his voice among the others? *Most sacrilegious murder.* Where, then, might he have gone? *The lord's annointed temple.* Not into the royal chamber – surely not. *Murder and treason!* Pray God, not into the royal chamber. *Death's counterfeit.* I had difficulty enough facing what I had done. *The great doom's image!* He will outright confess if he revisits the scene and sees his cousin's blood. *As from your graves!* I must rescue him again. *Ring the bell!* I must be the one who is strong enough for two.

A woman leaning down from a horse.
Two people who look exactly alike.
A stable-boy attacking a cornered rat.

Fillet of a fenny snake, in the cauldron boil and bake; eye of newt and toe of frog, wool of bat and tongue of dog, adder's fork and blind-worm's sting, lizard's leg and owlet's wing, for a charm of powerful trouble, like a hell-broth boil and bubble.

Smoke puffing out of a snow-covered chimney.
A porter holding his hand out to a guest.
A swineherd counting his new-born farrow.

Does a thought resemble a serpent?
Does a thought resemble a scorpion?
Is a thought simply a mirror inside the mind?

Turning the corner and coming upon the scene. *What's the business?* I trust that I look like a tired sleeper who has just been awakened. *Such a hideous trumpet.* If there is one little spot of blood, on either of our gowns or persons, we are both undone. *Calls to parley.* It is Macduff who holds the floor. *The sleepers of the house.* Why did my husband not take charge? *Not for you to hear.* He is the superior of Macduff – the better soldier. *Murder as it fell.* It is important to control the discourse. *Royal master's murdered!* We must be planting seeds in the minds of everyone here. *Woe, alas!* I do not see my husband anywhere. *What! In our house?* I do not dare to ask his whereabouts. I must wait until someone mentions where he has gone. Why would he leave when there is the taking-of-charge to do? Macduff will sway the crowd if we let him command the stage. *Too cruel anywhere!* I am finding this exhausting. *Contradict thyself!* My nerves are tuned to the highest stress. *Say it is not so!* They are starting to fray.

Terrified by my husband.
Falling onto the ground.

"A scorpion and another meet on the bank of a swift-moving stream! The scorpion asks the other for a ride on his back! The other asks, 'How can I be assured that you will not sting me?' 'We shall be one', the scorpion says! 'If you should drown then I shall surely drown as well!' The other is satisfied, and they set out to cross the stream, but in the midst the scorpion readies his fatal sting! 'I shall sting you,' says the scorpion to the other! 'I shall sting you and you shall surely drown!' The story is often told! At times in the telling, the other is a frog who is stung and who drowns! At other times in the telling, the other is a turtle with a hard, hard shell, and it is the scorpion alone who struggles in the water and drowns! In one of the tellings, the scorpion is blind!"

A woman whose thought is never for herself.
A woman who sacrifices her comfort for those in need.

The size of an infant - but what is not - whole corporeal being - the expense of his own - tending a wound - slit his regal throat - fools and incompetents - a creature digging hemlock - end this agony - control of a person's mind.

Banquo's wife. Lady Banquo. The mother of a young son.

Sitting on her horse in the courtyard. Looking down at me. Waiting for the entourage to assemble.

"The only thing I worry about is our son," she said. Her eyes showed great concern. "What would become of him if something should happen to us?"

"Steal a horse and the king cuts off an arm at the shoulder,"
said the man with only one arm.

My husband appears with Lennox. *An hour before this chance.* Where the devil has he been? *Liv'd a blessed time.* There is a spot of blood on his hand – between the index and the thumb! Put your hand behind your back! Draw attention away! *The wine of life is drawn.* My husband's palaver goes on and on! *The spring, the head, the fountain.* At least the blood is legitimate blood – thank God for that. Enough, my husband – you have said enough. *Repent me of my fury.* The more you talk, the more they listen. The more they listen, the more they think. *I did kill them.* The more you talk the more you are throwing our crowns away. *Wise, amazed, furious.* Make your point and then call to action. *My violent love.* Make your stamp on the clay of the mind and then lead the charge. *Silver skin lac'd.* You must tell them that Duncan's guards are the obvious culprits. *Colours of their trade.* You must plant the suspicion that it is the sons who stand to gain. *Who could refrain?* One word more and you shall be placing our heads on sharp poles.

Rumours about a queen who behaves like a ghost.
A torturer making a list of all his prisoners.
People huddling silently around their fires.

A cold day at the grave site! What will the boy do now? What a pity his mother is gone! Swept away at a shallow ford! A stumbling horse and she was gone! Banquo is sure that she hit her head on one of the rocks! A boy without a mother; a father without a wife; where is the justice? Banquo is probably the best of the men besides my husband! Macduff is a father to treasure, I'm sure, as well! None of the others would do to raise a son alone! The boy seems lost beside the grave site! I almost feel like taking his hand! What is the matter with Duncan's wife? Can she not understand her role as the reigning Queen? She is snivelling under a blanket and wiping her nose! My husband has always admired Banquo! We should bring him in on the plan! As long as he sees how his thread will add shade to the tapestry! The country needs a warrior king! Each call to parley makes us weaker! Scotland is slowly bleeding away! I am sure that Banquo and Macduff will fall into line! Perhaps Banquo's son – young Fleance, this splendid boy – could follow my husband!

"Some talk of Malcolm and Donalbain, some talk of Macbeth."
"All the rumours seem to agree that King Duncan is dead."

One fierce foray - it is not known - the day of all my days - you have baffled me - stories of the times - circles inside circles - cleanse the stuff'd bosom - read the human threads - favoured with a son - our bloods had not commingled.

Well, sleep is the great restorative. The healing agent of all life's sores. You have said so many times yourself.

We must change our routine somehow. Less time at court, perhaps. Would it help if we went riding in the afternoons?

We could look for that meadow again. Surely it can't be far from the castle. It would be pleasant to spend some time there again.

Two scorpions met a frog on the bank of a river.
"Will you carry us on your back?," the two scorpions asked.

Macduff is quick to challenge. *O! By whom?* I did not think of Macduff as so able to command. *Wherefore did you so?* I thought of him as a loving father. *Help me hence, ho!* A courtier of Duncan. – A man for the palace but not for the field. *Look to the lady.* Now he is cornering my husband like a stable rat. *Hold our tongues.* I must draw attention away. *Claim this argument.* My husband is speaking too long. *Should be spoken.* Even I am not quite convinced – and I am his wife. *Hid in an auger-hole.* He was not born to be a player – he can only play himself. *Look to the lady.* Let my faint be the welcome curtain which ends the bad speech.

Bent trees

grow
bent.

Two animals held together by a yoke.
A person telling another person a story.
Water gurgling around a rock in a shallow ford.

Straight trees
grow
straight.

"The scorpion mating ritual commences with the pair performing a dance called the 'Promenade À Deux'."

What is the force
that bends these trees
or leaves them alone?

Is a mind a miniature kingdom?
Does it suffer from civil war?
Can a thought kill its king and seize the throne?

They are carrying me up the stairway to our chamber. I shall revive at the top of the stairs and thank them all. What if they see inside our room? There might be drops of blood on the floor! Surely we closed the secret door to the secret passage? In past days, I would have been certain my lord has done all that needs be done. Now, I can't be sure what is left undone. I cannot keep thinking for two. The burden is more than I can heft. I cannot continue to carry such weight uphill. I awake and sigh and ask where am I now. Please put me down. I need fresh air. I shall walk on the parapet for a while. It is a terrible thing that has happened. All our sympathy to his sons. Scotland has suffered a terrible loss. My husband was ever a strong admirer of Duncan as king.

Chapter 9

Macbeth 5

My Banquo and his Fleance. Standing and talking in the courtyard. *Thou hast it now.* Waiting for the grooms to prepare the horses. *The weird women promised.* The last parley of father and son before the deluge. *Play'dst most foully.* What father does not have thoughts that he dare not share with his son? *Stand in thy posterity.* What subject does not have thoughts that he dare not share with his sovereign? *Should be the root and father.* I do not need to read your lips, my friend – I know what you are thinking. I place myself in your place and I think my Banquo thoughts and I listen in. *Set me up in hope.* Talk to your son in endless palaver – keep your silences with me. *But hush! no more.* You squelched me when I asked for time alone.

To be the hand

Three people standing and talking in a courtyard.
A woman rubbing the temples of a man.
A country market counter piled with goods.

which plants and waters

"The people of Scotland are no different from the people of any other land.
They want a couple of chickens and perhaps a cow."

the seeds of time.

What can you get for friendship at the market?
Where is the counter where such things are bartered and sold?
Is loyalty the cheapest thing for sale?

Closely questioning Banquo. *Ride you this afternoon?* What questions is he asking while answering me? *Hold a solemn supper.* What are you thinking, my old friend, Banquo? *My genius is rebuked.* Why did you question the witches so closely when they met us? *Father to a line of kings.* Why did you chide me by saying, You shall be king? *Is't far you ride?* Did you relish me saying, Your children shall yet be kings? *A barren sceptre in my gripe.* Did you smirk as we rode along, side by side? Did you tell yourself that our ride together was temporary? *Goes Fleance with you?* That our engagement, as captains, was soon to come to an end? *Fail not our great feast.* The difference my friend, is that you trust the witches to plant and water all the seeds of time, while I have reached out and snatched my seeds alone from their hands.

Nurses rocking cradles in a nursery.
A master-weaver drawing diagrams of a tapestry.
An elderly lady spinning wool.

Riding out with my son twixt court time and feast time! As much as will fill up the time betwixt now and then! These are early times, my son! No need to act the racing courier on your very first ride! Let the horse be your guide on such a leisurely outing! When the times are urgent, then give him a taste of your spur! It is pleasant here in the glade! I had a thought to catch up to Banquo and his son, Fleance, but no matter! Better we take our time and let you learn to ride! Best rest easy in the saddle, bring your rhythm up from the stirrups, merge your mind with the mind of the horse as much as you can! You will prove to be a master! Riding to you is mother's milk, I can plainly see! Remember the rocking horse you so often used to ride?

"I hear no talk of holding an election whatsoever."
"There is a pressing need for stability in the land."

Inside the human mind - crying out for release - to draw suspicion away - struts and frets his hour - a stool overturned - the foolish strategy - the lingering wounds - keep constant watch - the other side of the fence - savage adventurers.

Talk of the future is not for me. I have learned to not think of the future. I find the present day enough of a challenge for me.

I want a mind which is devoid of speculation. Yesterday is the bog behind me. Tomorrow the hill ahead.

You ask what would have become of us if we had never met. From such heights the wisest among us lose their footing and fall. Better for both of us to leave such questions aside.

Soon every peasant in the kingdom wore a crown.
Every peasant thought himself to be a king.

Giving instructions to the murderers. *Held you so under fortune.* Oh you brazen, brazen fools. Do you not realize that you shall be witnesses? *Know that Banquo was your enemy.* Do you not know that I am scorching the land in the wake of my campaign? *Every minute of his being.* Will you leave behind widows and orphans? *With barefaced power.* If so, the prospect pleases. I would feed you to my dogs, were I to think so ill of my dogs as to feed them such chuff.

Bidding farewell to Banquo.
Instructing the murderers.

I see that you get along right well with Fleance! He is a boy who will make an excellent soldier some day! I told your mother to be sure to honour Banquo, tonight, at the banquet! To present him eminence with hand and with eye! You know we have been partners in many a battle! It was he who helped me to push Norway into the sea! He was on my flank when I unseamed the traitor, Macdonwald – from the nave to the chaps! We shared equally in the king's remembrance when we met him in the field! Whoa! Let us walk them for a while! Let your horse cool off, every so often, whenever you ride! A good horse, with reasonable pacing, can stay the course! He will ride for hours upon hours if you treat him right!

A man who bests every challenger in battle.
A man who pledges loyalty to his king.

Lesson of the battlefield - your faulty battle plan - fear in the eyes - the life to come - to see what is done - a man who chokes - such a fusion - already begun the siege - utter a single word - drifting off in the dark.

Our defenses fell into disrepair. At every parley, Duncan gave a piece of Scotland away. I was almost relieved when the Norwegians invaded our shores.

Duncan received much praise for sending Macdonwald to parley with Sweno. All the thanes expressed their relief at the news of the accord with the invaders. Who remembers that I alone opposed the king?

I faced Sweno on the beach and drove him back to Norway. I faced Macdonwald eye to eye and gutted him stem to stern. All of this to save my cousin's shrinking throne.

They struggled and stumbled on land.
They almost drowned themselves in the water.

The queen is on her throne. *Scotch'd the snake, not kill'd it.* She is delegating tasks to her many servants. *Malice remains in danger.* She is regal as she organizes the daily operations of the enterprise. *The frame of things disjoint.* She is imperial in the way she directs her staff. *Eat our meal in fear.* I shall wait until she is finished. *The affliction of these terrible dreams.* I am idle until tonight. *The torture of the mind.* Her concentration on task is a soothing balm to my forehead and my mind. *Life's fitful fever.* Perhaps she will rub my temples when she has time.

A man asking another a series of questions.
A fire snapping and crackling under a cauldron.
A father teaching his son to ride a horse.

Thrice the brinded cat hath mew'd. Thrice and once the hedge-pig whined. Harpier cries 'tis time, 'tis time. Round about the cauldron go; in the poison'd entrails throw. Toad, that under cold stone days and nights has thirty-one; swelter'd venom sleeping got, boil thou first i' the charmed pot. Double, double toil and trouble; fire burn, and cauldron bubble.

Children who fear that their parents will not come home.
Spears and longbows stacked against a fortress wall.
A torturer having supper with his family.

What do we trade for a hungry stomach?
What do we trade for a hungry mind?
What do we offer instead of coins to balance the scale?

And what to tell my lady love? *Your remembrance apply to Banquo.* What shall I tell the love of my life? *O, full of scorpions is my mind, dear wife.* That she has everything, now, that together we have always wanted. *Ere the bat hath flown.* That she has a palace of her own in a kingdom so large and powerful that nothing can assail herself and what is hers. *Black Hecate's summons.* Concern yourself with banquets and place-cards and orders of comings and goings and nothing else whatever, my innocent love. *A deed of dreadful note.* One of us should enjoy this moment we have come to in our dreams. *Be innocent of the knowledge.* Only one of us need suffer from now on. *Tear to pieces that great bond.* When I need a moment of peace, I shall leave the thoughts of my mind behind and think of you and what you are thinking – of the placing of your guests at your banquets – and I shall have respite. *Make strong themselves by ill.* We are partners who can now divide our tasks.

Deciding to keep my secret.
Protecting my loving wife.

You are riding well, my son! You are easy in the saddle – a very good sign! All this countryside you see belongs to us now! Not only the grounds of our castle, but all of Scotland! Every blade of grass and every single tree! And we shall leave it all to you – your mother and I! Between the two of us we shall make you a proper prince! I shall tell the nobles early that you are my heir! Well, here we are at the castle! Let us here dismount! It is a long way round to the stables, but we shall walk the horses ourselves, notwithstanding the grooms! Always remember your horse's welfare! Your horse must always be walked until cooled! You depend upon him as he depends on you! A moment, my son! Here, take my reins as well! I see some men with whom I must have a brief talk! I shall only be a moment! I must ask them if Banquo and Fleance have returned!

A man whose word cannot be trusted.
A man for whom friendship is a knife in the back.

Their credulous story - hewing beams - of ravens and hawks - pluck from the memory - unfortunate trick of fate - lost our way - places each foot carefully - a raging fever - no human being - praying on a battlefield.

I used to lie awake and stare at the ceiling. Were my victories making Duncan, the inadequate, look kingly? Was I moving myself further away from the crown?

How wrong to think that my deeds stood out on their own. My valorous deeds and Duncan's failed diplomacy side by side? I was thunderstruck when Duncan made Malcolm the next king.

Hours of brooding, my love. Hours of commiserating with you. I used to ask the old dog what he thought I should do.

"What can I steal and be rewarded for?"
asked the man with only one arm.

The great captain of the realm. *A light, a light!* How many times have I been faced by three cowardly slaves? Desperation is on your face. *Tis he.* You are more concerned with your boy than with your own welfare! You have made the classic mistake of the apprentice hand. *Stand to't.* Take care of yourself on the battlefield and let the other soldiers take care of themselves as well. Fight the fight which appears in front of you; fight the slave who threatens your life; your fellow-soldier will do the same and you both shall live. *It will be rain to-night.* But once play the Good Samaritan, and both you and your fellow will feel the plunge of the knives in both your backs. Your day will be done before the battle is long commenced. *Let it come down.* I stab you in the back as you hold Fleance by the doublet. Your sword remains in your scabbard. *O, treach-*

ery! Oh, Banquo, my former friend! Did you think that the wars were over? It seems the witches have bred complacency in you. *Fly, good Fleance, fly, fly, fly!* The blood gushes out on my hands. *Thou mayst revenge.* You turn to me as you fall. Do you know the face of your knife-bearer? *O slave!* It is no mind. Plenty of time, where you are going, to make review of your faulty battle-plan.

Oat cakes sizzling in an iron pan.
A shoemaker hammering a tack into a boot.
A boy learning to say his ABCs.

What do the witches want for this kingdom? They were wise, no doubt, to cast the feeble Duncan aside! But did the witches not know of the battle? Could not they measure the regal bearings of Banquo and myself? It was I who unseamed Macdonwald! It was I who devised the plan! Banquo was merely in support – in holding my flank! Why promote another Duncan – a whole series of Duncan-like kings? Can they not see what Scotland needs? Let milkmaids churn the butter; let kitchen-boys sweep the floor! Their predictions are a call to parley, not to war!

"Macbeth will be a firm hand on the tiller."
"He is the warrior who turned back the Norwegian tide."

Much more amenable - heavenly protection - the poorest decision - want to know why - no porter at the gates - where is the justice - the charm of an adder - beyond your scope - pristine streams - always been of one mind.

I study you sometimes when you are asleep. Perhaps you study me when I am asleep. Very few such moments come to either of us two.

We have arrived at a fork in the road. Voices call to each of us. There is a force which seems to determine what we hear.

There is the warp and there is the weft. We, each of us, have made our contribution. We each have chosen different threads for our tapestry.

"I can only carry one," the frog replied.
"Me first!" said both scorpions together.

I turn away from Banquo. His corpse is safe for all time. His blood is mingling with the mud in the soggy ground. *Who did strike out the light?* The others have the boy surrounded. His horse is calming down. *Wast not the way?* He keeps kicking it in the ribs but it stands still. I reach out and grasp his doublet from behind. Come here, you young whelp. I will teach you how to ride. This ride with your father shall be the ride of your life. *There's but one down.* The horse bolts as he kicks it. The fools let go of the reins to save themselves. *The son is fled.* The boy gives me a wallop with his hand. *We have lost best half.* I lose my grip on his doublet and he slips from my grasp. *Well, let's away, and say.* The horse kicks up the sand as it gallops away.

A serpent
will shun
a scorpion.

A climber losing his footing on the side of a cliff.
Coloured threads weaving through a tapestry.
A sword splitting a man from stem to stern.

A scorpion
will shun
a snake.

"The male scorpion injects a small amount of his venom into the female as a means of pacification."

Only inside
the human mind
do they share a cause.

Sell the baskets we brought to market?
Sell the mule we need to ride home?
What can we truthfully say is definitely not for sale?

So Fleance is escaped. *Then comes my fit again.* I had him in my grasp and he slipped away. *Thy children shall be kings.* I had his doublet in this fist and was about to yank him from his horse and plunge this dagger into his throat and he slipped away. *In time will venom breed.* This is almost supernatural. Into air. – Into thin air. How can one have something in one's hand – as corporeal as the rock on which I stand – and find it disappear in the space of an instant?

Chapter 10

Lady Macbeth 5

The first of many fine days at court. *Here's our chief guest.* All the splendour of the aura of the crown. *Gap in our great feast.* The Macbeths, Lord and Lady – King and Queen. *An all-thing unbecoming.* I read the faces – read the faces – as we pass. *Ride you this afternoon?* Healing is the word of action for the day. *Is't far you ride?* My lord speaks at length with his good friend, Banquo. *Fail not our feast.* We have our Banquo's support at least. *Goes Fleance with you?* I shall work on Lady Macduff. I shall bring her into the fold. *Master of his time.* My lord must work his spell on Macduff and such others as failed to make the journey to Scone.

To be the tapestry

One old friend talking quietly with another.
A meadow with flowers and a gentle breeze.
A queen sitting unnoticed on a splendid throne.

which weaves the threads

"The people of Scotland are no different from the people of any other land.
They want the crops to grow so there will be harvest aplenty."

of the course of the day.

How well do we know our own thoughts?
Do we think about our thoughts?
Do our thoughts think about us?

I had no desire to sit alone on this throne. That was never any portion of the plan. *Nought's had, all's spent.* My lord is in the room, but I lack his presence. He huddles at the foot of the throne room with the kind of beings who excite disgust. What can be so very important as to parley with these men? *Our desire is got.* Now they walk out onto the parapet. I cannot see them now. I dare not go to the door and listen in. I would never spy on my husband. – He would never spy on me. *Got without content.* We share every thought that is ever in our heads. *Dwell in doubtful joy.* The sound of horses in the courtyard. Has my husband gone with these men? Where, now, I wonder, is Macbeth?

A congregation praying for victory over its foes.
Nobles who shun the investiture of their king.
Whinnying horses lying wounded on a battlefield.

Sitting alone in the throne room! The servants come and go! Every footstep makes a sound! Hustle and bustle in preparation for the next affair of state! Steady traffic back and forth to the banquet room! The old dog lies so peacefully! Not the twitch of a paw disturbs the old fellow's sleep! Where oh where has my husband gone? The servants can't seem to find him! He has been keeping apart of late! Spending more and more time alone! There is much that I would like to discuss with him!

"Rumours of Malcolm and Donalbain."
"Rumours of Banquo and Macduff."

What is a little blood - a walking shadow - what holds you back - heads on poles - the way sideways - setting out place-names - out of our control - a trick of the landscape - to keep them dry - able to see by the candle.

Sometimes I think that I became you and you became me. So we were still two people rather than simply one. As if our bloods had not commingled at all.

I look at you. And I look at me. And I wonder, what makes us the same?, what makes us different?

What would a child take from us two? What leave behind? That is why everyone seeks the first glimpse of a new-born child.

But the king was not so generous as the peasants imagined.
The king was the only one in the kingdom to wear a sword.

My husband is only as strong as I. I am only as strong as he. I cannot believe that he will further act without me. We have always been of one mind in our enterprise. Why such questioning of our friend? I could never believe he would strike at the Banquo family. As monarchs we shall need as strong support as we can gather. Count the thanes, my lord. – Count the thanes. It is a mathematical certainty: if one subtracts and never adds, one is due for a fall. Remove the legs from your stool and you end up on the floor.

Sitting alone on my throne.
Sensing the weight of the crown.

Sitting on the throne! The throne is empty beside me! I asked the waiting women to bring my new diadem! The servants come and go! Polishing candlesticks and dusting walls! Making up fires and removing the ash! Brushing the cobwebs out of the tapestry! The man who is making the fireplace ready is working quite diligently! From time to time his boy brings in a bundle of firewood! The girl with the duster who didn't see me got quite a start! She almost stepped upon my toe before I coughed and cleared my throat! The echo makes this room seem very large! My husband has been absent for quite some time!

A woman who is cruel to her servants.
A woman who always breaks her word.

Vaulting ambition - which accurately weighs - its essence, not its aura - to a mind diseased - toppled a kingdom - a runaway horse - how we are seen - the fate in the adage - dwell in the lowest circle - looked after each other.

I did not see what you saw at the banquet. I was guessing all the time what it could possibly be. All that I could see, the whole time, was an empty stool.

I was counting on the good will of all our new subjects. I had all the cards made up – with everyone in their proper places. I wanted everything to be settled from that night on.

I had never been on a battlefield. But I knew that we must remain calm. I thought that you would be the one to anchor me.

The hawk saw the frog and the mouse yoked together.
They will make one excellent meal thought the hawk.

My husband once said that Fleance would make, one day, a fine and stout young warrior. That Banquo, as tutor, would prove well enough for the average candidate, but that he – himself, Macbeth – would be best to train the lad. My lord has a life-time of military lore that Banquo – the faithful plough horse – will never know. He says that Banquo is plodding and steady – in following orders right through to the end – and that he would rather have Banquo to take up his flank than Macduff. Macduff can raise an army, for sure, but Macduff's support is numbers, nothing more. When the battle rages, it is

Banquo's banner – through the smoke and the mist and the noise – that brings welcome relief. Macduff is the one best left at home – so my husband always says – or at court.

A stool overturned in a banquet room.
Two people whispering in the privacy of their chamber.
A midwife displaying a new-born child.

Hail! Hail! Hail! Lesser than Macbeth, and greater. Not so happy, yet much happier. Thou shalt get kings, though thou be none: so all hail, Macbeth and Banquo! Banquo and Macbeth, all hail!

Two women gathering flowers in a meadow.
A little girl playing with her dolls.
French wine being poured into sparkling glasses.

Are we what we think?
Are we what we do?
Are we what we wish to be and do?

How can these servants spend such hours in this room? And how does one draw their attention when a missive requires to be sent? *Say to the king.* So Banquo is gone from the court. And Fleance, his son, has gone with him. And if Banquo and Fleance ride, does my husband ride too? *Attend his leisure.* I am asking in regards to the banquet which we are preparing. *A few words.* I want everyone here by the time the proceedings begin. *Madam, I will.* I want everyone here on time – no exceptions allowed.

Sending to know of Banquo.
Sending to know of Macbeth.

I asked my husband to sit and share my joy! Place the crown on your head and look around you and smile! Enjoy what we have achieved for a day or two! Let us take one day to bask in the glow which our valiant efforts have made! This is the moment we imagined when we first began to talk! After a rest there will be time to make further plans! Keep in mind our pledge to do everything together! Remember that we are partners of head and of heart! No, this is not the place to talk, I quite agree! But we can do so, at any time, in the privacy of our chamber! We have barely been together since we have been crowned!

A woman who has grown distant from her husband.
A woman who does not deserve to raise a child.

Read behind the eyes - smother'd in surmise - glean whatever is possible - rumours seem to agree - come what come may - such small flaws - give an ultimatum - if I could only know - see how far you get - to enlighten our way.

The banquet room. Our first event as king and queen. Long before the time for festivities to commence.

The room was completely empty. There was just myself and the girl. We were setting the place-cards at the appropriate places.

"What do you think of this?" I asked. "That I leave an empty stool, and a place-card, in memory of Banquo's wife and the mother of his son? Would such a gesture – do you think – be a good idea?"

"Steal the king's crown and it will be placed upon your head."

At last we sit together on the throne. *You keep alone.* Being alone so much is not good for you my husband. *Should indeed have died.* You are never in the court, it seems, these days. *Frame of things disjoint.* It is important that all things now return to normal. *Eat our meal in fear.* There has been enough agitation. *Terrible dreams.* We must bring the whole realm together in quiet and peace. *Torture of the mind.* That is the theme of the banquet tonight. *Restless ecstasy.* You must play the comforting host. *Bright and jovial.* You must allay all fears of chaos and confusion.

A king lying in bedclothes soaked in blood.
Four torturers lashing a man to a wagon wheel.
Laymen hurrying to fortify a church.

A word with you, Lady Macduff, if I might make so bold! A word or two, between us, before you go! I sense that your husband is in a hurry! He seemed a little abrupt just now! No doubt he is anxious to ride post-haste to Scone! My husband is counting on his presence! They've been so compatible in the past! Their regard for each other will increase in the days to come! I have always admired your family! You are so lucky to have your children! They seem to be with you all the time! Your son resembles his father in every way! I grew up in a very close family! My father always wanted a son! I enjoyed overhearing you banter with your boy! Please tell the servant to say that you are occupied for the moment! Your husband will countenance, I am sure, a slight delay! It is so pleasant here in the sunshine! What is a moment or two on such a splendid morning? I shall rely on you in the future! You will come to Scone of course? I shall be ever so pleased to have a good chat at Scone!

"There are rumours of tensions at the new court."
"Who is close with King Macbeth and who is outside."

What goes on - talk of future greatness - the day will come - plague upon the land - know who I am - so they can talk - the one to anchor me - pressing need for stability - we shall be one - cut out its tongue.

Once in a while, some light comes in at the window. There is very little light outside. The darkness makes the days all seem the same.

There is such an echo in here. Yet when I call out to the servants, they don't seem to hear. Sometimes I wonder whether all of them are deaf.

The room is always so draughty and so cold. The tapestry – which we have ordered to hang on the wall – won't be ready, it seems, for quite some time. Would you consider, my love, moving the thrones – the two of them, of course – to a smaller room?

Two scorpions lay dead on the bank of a river.
A frog swam alone to the other side.

Why so much thought of Banquo? *Remembrance apply to Banquo.* Surely Banquo has never been tempted to tamper with fate. *Vizards to our hearts.* You have fought together in battles. *You must leave this.* It was Banquo who held your flank. *Full of scorpions is my mind.* We need strong alliances now, not suspicious division. *Banquo and his Fleance.* You must bring Macduff back to court. *Copy's not eterne.* Find out why he does not attend. *Comfort yet.* You must give no more thought to Banquo – do you hear me, my lord? *A deed of dreadful note.* Do you remember you spoke of Fleance as almost your son?

Grace
before
dinner.

A master-warrior training a lad to use a spear.
A man gnashing his teeth in the grip of sleep.
A very large room with a hollow echo.

Prayers
before
murder.

"Once the mating is complete, the male scorpion will retreat in order to avoid being cannibalized by the female."

Remorse
before
God.

Are we what people think of us?
Are we what is done to us?
Are we what others wish for us to be?

I asked my love to go out riding the other day. *What's to be done?* He put me off – for pressing business – but he promised that we would do so one fine morning. *Innocent of the knowledge.* Where is that meadow, I wonder, where we walked on the day that we met? *Dearest chuck.* It must be here about the castle. *Applaud the deed.* I remember a few-hours ride. *Sealing night.* The crowns and robes are our public achievement. – They bring stability to the realm. *The tender eye.* What we need now is a balm to sooth our minds. *Bloody and invisible hand.* We have not yet reached perfection. The meadow cannot be far from the castle. *Tear to pieces that great bond.* If we could go there again, I am sure we would both feel fulfilled.

Chapter 11

Macbeth 6

This banquet is more for my wife than for myself. *Your own degrees.* I welcome everyone to my wife's fine home. *At first and last.* It will give her peace – me none. *Hearty welcome.* She counts those who are here tonight. – I count those who are absent. *Ourself will mingle.* The absentees will receive my greetings before too long. *Play the humble host.* I wonder whether Banquo has been losing so much sleep as I have done? *Keeps her state.* Can one contemplate the future and nod by the fire? *Be large in mirth.* Has he been smiling in his rocking chair as young Fleance makes paper crowns, while the witches toil in the mud and the blood for his sake? *The table round.* Well Banquo, this much is for certain. You shall find good sleep tonight at the end of your trail.

To be the goblet

Servants setting the table for a banquet.
A fox closely pursued by baying hounds.
The crashing of an ear-splitting drum.

which drinks the health

"The people of Scotland are no different from the people of any other land.
They want to pray to God on Sunday and before every meal."

of the entire kingdom.

What is the purpose of a banquet?
Why the toasts and the meat and the drink?

Why the scraps thrown into the rushes to feed the dogs?

Welcoming all to my wife's fine banquet. *Here I'll sit in the midst.* My scruffy friends wave me over to the door. *There's blood upon thy face.* Well Banquo you sleep well, but your son has found no such comfort. *T'is Banquo's then.* Fleance will be the witches' darling until my dogs have run him down. *His throat is cut.* Even now he hears the trumpets and the hounds. *Fleance is safe.* Think of your son in the mud and the rain tonight as I drink pledges to you. *Then comes my fit again.* He is hiding in a foxhole and dreaming of crowns. *Cabin'd, cribb'd, confined.* My wife restores me to my place. *Doubts and fears.* Well, the son has managed more than has the father – in defeat, he has struck a saucy blow.

A man and woman, hand in hand, in a meadow.
Boar, venison, deer and rabbit on a spit.
A girl tossing grain to a gaggle of geese.

Pausing beside a river of blood! An impediment in my journey across the land! Sitting on the bank! Bloodied up to my waist as I tried to cross! No stepping stones to utilize! No raftsman as at Acheron! No frog to offer to carry me along on his back! The slope is alarmingly steep! The current is dangerously strong! What to do, I wonder! I have come a long way so far! All my gains I have in my backpack! I shall lose them if I turn back! Going back would be as tedious as go o'er!

"I hear that all is going to be well."
"All the thanes are coming together to hold a great feast."

Pay a heavy price - what he thinks he sees - brief candle - snared two souls - at the highest level - a diamond in the depths - a sudden opening in the earth - confusion in the realm - ranked in the chronicle - to wash in the dark.

I am worried about you, my love. Hence the doctor, hence the nurse. Hence these other watchers of your welfare.

Turn the peg of a musical instrument far beyond where it was designed to go and the strings will snap. This is you, my love. This is you.

We have become the cat and the dog. Each is a different form of being. Each has earned his rightful place by the warmth of the fire.

"Let us drink each other's blood," said one witch to another.
"We shall be as one until the end of time."

My wife, my wife, my wife. *You do not give the cheer.* Always the guide in matters domestic. *Our country's honour roofed.* A pledge to Banquo – to wonderful Banquo – would he were here. *The grac'd person of our Banquo.* Everyone drinks to the gracious Banquo – who fails our feast. *Pleas't your highness to grace us.* I look for a stool among my guests, who vie for me to grace them with my presence. *The table's full.* But what is this? – What is this? – What is this? *Where?* How could anyone not know a stool from what I see? *Which of you have done this?* Were twenty gashes not enough? *Thou cans't not say I did it.* Have you come back here from the grave? *Never shake thy gory locks at me.* What do you want with me? They told me you were dead! *Dare look on that.* Why do you not carry a sword? *Appal the devil.* I could understand your intent if you brandished a sword.

Welcoming the guests.
Whispering with the murderers.

Stepping into the river of blood! Determined to cross or gladly perish! Quickly sinking to my knees and then my thighs! Pushing drifting corpses aside! Grinning skulls and scattered bones! All of them sweeping swiftly along in the rushing tide! The current grows stronger as I wade! Threatening to rip my pack away! Threatening to sweep away all I have won so far! The blood is rising to my chest! The blood is rising to my chin! I choose my footing carefully! The slope goes down and down! I pause as the blood is frothing at my lips!

A man who engages with evil spirits.
A man who snuffs out lives as one would snuff a candle.

We still have judgment - more and more and more - earned his rightful place - if something should happen - a gentle breeze - grim silence - bread on the table - the faithful plough horse - the depths of this cave - the conquered and the conqueror.

Macduff – who had praised my valour – supported Malcolm. Banquo – who had fought beside me – supported Malcolm. Every thane had left a dagger in my back.

To live in a Scotland devoid of hope. To live in a Scotland devoid of valour. These foolish thanes had drained my joy away.

Duncan's sons were callow lightweights. Neither warriors nor diplomats. The kingdom, now on its knees, would soon be prone.

An old man and a boy stood on a hillside.
It is not known which was the first to speak.

My wife arrives to comfort me. *Painting of your fear.* She holds my head in her hands and rubs my temples. *The air-drawn dagger.* If I could only know her secret. *A woman's story.* How does she keep such cold command? *Such faces.* I have never been one to yield in military conflict. *But on a stool.* Why do I flinch under conflict now? *Why what care I?* In armed conflict, I saw my moment and spoke with my sword. *Speak too.* I stride back across the room and confront the stool. *Charnel houses and our graves.* If any such ghosts want to face Macbeth, they must deal with me. *Those that we bury.* It is the lesson of the battlefield. *The maws of kites.* I show my claws and the ghost retreats and disappears.

A sprinkling of thorns on a pathway.
A traveller adjusting his backpack.
A scorpion sleeping peacefully on a log.

A drum, a drum! Macbeth doth come. The weird sisters, hand in hand, posters of the sea and land, thus do go about, about: thrice to thine and thrice to mine and thrice again, to make up nine. Peace! the charm's wound up. All hail, Macbeth! hail to thee, Thane of Glamis! All hail, Macbeth, hail to thee, Thane of Cawdor! All hail, Macbeth, thou shalt be king hereafter!

A look-out taking an arrow in the eye.
Daggers which probe the backs of former friends.
Roving gangs stealing sheep and cattle and horses.

Why the gathering of all and sundry?
Why the checking of swords at the door?
Why the ready acceptance of each one's proper degree?

This is the milk of human kindness that my wife has told me about. I saw Duncan as my king and my cousin. I saw Banquo as the captain of my flank. I saw Fleance as a stripling who would make a stout man some day. Such thought as this has made it hard to cut them down. It is my wife who babbles on in tones that are best left in the past. What care I what Lady Macduff has said to her son? That Macduff refers to his chickens and their dam? If Banquo's wife leaves a boy without nurture – if Banquo's son is bereft at her funeral – why what care I? Mother's milk is only of service to babes in arms. The world is much more amenable to tooth and claw. I can no longer think of these people as human beings. I must see them as Hyrcan tigers or Russian bears.

Confronting Banquo's ghost.
Facing a river of blood.

Opening my lips! Tasting the blood which bubbles there! Seeking entrance to my being! Welcome in! Tasting blood and liking the taste! Taking a swallow and feeling fine! Satisfaction far beyond the finest wine! Feeling my whole corporeal being rise in stature! Gaining strength with every swallow! Rising up to enormous size! Taller than the highest hills in the kingdom! Taller than Scotland ever bid me, before, to be! Towering over the petty English epicures! Growing in stature with every swallow! Why did I hesitate to cross? The secret is to drink of the river of blood!

A man who slaughters women and innocent children.
A man who drinks the witches' brew as mother's milk.

Fail to see the rage - as for the murders - our little broken boy - canst thou not minister - his trusting guest - the immediate threat - there are none - devil speak true - cut the contenders down - i worry about you.

As for the murders, my dear. As for the series of gruesome murders. Why try to treat a disease with no known cure?

They would never have let us live. They would never have let us prosper. Duncan, Malcolm, Banquo and Macduff – each one of them was sharpening his knife.

I solved the Duncan problem. I solved the Banquo problem. In a day or two, I shall settle with Macduff.

The king grew more and more sad as each day passed.
The princess watched him grow despondent day by day.
The peasants were suffering from a plague upon the land.

My wife as my perpetual rescuer. It seems she continues to speak. *Your noble friends do lack you.* The lady who keeps an even keel in the breast of the waves. *I drink to the general joy.* So cool inside her armour on such a sweltering day. *Our dear friend Banquo.* Again my pledge to the absent Banquo. *Would he were here.* Again comes this terrible fiend. *To all, and him, we thirst.* Again, covered in blood and shaking his head. *Avaunt, and quit my sight!* Again, covered in mud and pointing at me. *Let the earth hide thee!* Know you not that I have no remorse? *Thy bones are marrowless!* Know you not that I have no regrets? *Thy blood is cold!* You were a fallen tree on the path to a better Scotland. *No speculation in those eyes.* Your descendants are thorns on the way ahead. *Thou dost glare.* Everyone here knows why you are dead and drinks to that cause.

A doctor leaning over a sleeping patient.
A woman chopping vegetables for a stew.
A man and a boy working a cross-cut saw.

These three weird sisters cannot be real! They are figments of my mind! The conjurings of a sideshow! A moment's distraction! No more real than the ghost of Banquo! Why these witches, ghosts and scorpions – it is my thoughts which bring them to life! It is my thoughts which dismiss them again! When I turn on them they run and hide like thieves! All things are made by thought! There is nothing outside of man which he doesn't create! So there, my three fine friends! I shall direct you next time we meet! You shall take your marching instructions from my command!

"The guilty have fled the kingdom and we are free of their treachery."
"Only a few disgruntled thanes fail to acknowledge the new king."

Steal a horse - absent for quite some time - the shaping of this game - not yet reached perfection - a lightning strike - frog swam alone - penetrate the skin - plague the inventor - the clay of the mind - a surge of certainty.

I had to look clear down to the bottom of my mind. I had to make an assessment of what I was and what I wanted to be. Then I snuffed out one candle and lit another.

I only had to stifle half of myself. I didn't have to murder the whole being. There was a moment after which I was never the same.

I was Glamis and then I was Cawdor. I was Cawdor and then I was king. I was Macbeth and then – I was Macbeth.

A baby witch grew curious.
She watched her mother as the cauldron bubbled and boiled.

My wife attempts to hold me and rub my temples. *What man dare, I dare.* I cannot let you touch me. *The rugged Russian bear.* In your presence I feel myself sinking beneath the waves. *The armed rhinoceros.* What you have done, my wife, has been impeccable. *The Hyrcan tiger.* What you have not been able to do, no mortal woman could do. *My firm nerves shall never tremble!* Dragging your husband up the slope before the engulfment of the tide has been exhausting for you. *Hence horrible shadow!* I must release you from your burden. *Unreal mockery!* I must relieve you of your cares. *Hence!* I will hoist my backpack on my back and strike out alone.

The eyes in the sky
are
a faery tale.

A man attempting to ford a raging river.
A musician mending broken strings.
A man with many daggers in his back.

The eyes in the dark
are
an old woman's yarn.

"The scorpion is perceived both as an embodiment of evil and a protective force that counters evil."

At the eyes
inside the head
it is dangerous to scoff.

Why does it mean to speak for all present?
What does it mean to drink one's health?
Why do we shed a tear at the prospect of an empty stool?

What now, my love, what now? *It will have blood.* My wife, where have you led me? *Blood will have blood.* You peered a little way into the cave but did not go in. *Stones have been known to move.* You cannot prattle of young Fleance, alone at his mother's grave. *Trees to speak.* And of Lady Macduff and her charming, chirping brood. *To the weird sisters.* And of Duncan's snivelling wife offering you a seat by the fire on a cold, bleak, stormy night of a bloody campaign. *Bent to know.* And still hold out your hand where the adder is known to sting. *By the worst means.* So you ask me about Macduff. *For mine own good.* Let us say that I have sent to him to parley, as Duncan used to do with all the enemies who surrounded him, from without Scotland and from within. *In blood stepped in so far.* Yes, my love, we are both short of sleep. *Have in head.* We shall soon have sleep aplenty. *Will to hand.* The scorpion sleeps when his venom has been discharged.

Chapter 12

Lady Macbeth 6

This banquet will be the crowning moment. The coronation was an awkward and ill-attended event. The stunning nature of Duncan's death made the ceremony somewhat less than it should have been. We – both of us – were glad to have it over and done. But tonight is the inauguration of the tranquility which everyone desires. No more of the uncertainty by which the frequent invasions and the constant negotiations have plagued our kingdom for so long. I do not see Lady Macduff. – I do not see Lady Macduff. Perhaps the waiting women have seen her. I have not seen Lady Macduff since the hasty departure of everyone on the occasion of Duncan's demise.

To be the diadem

A queen and a servant setting out place-names.
A person carefully reaching a hand to a dog.
A group of people raising glasses in a toast.

which offers peace

"The people of Scotland are no different from the people of any other land.
They want their children to have a place to grow in the sunshine."

to the troubled realm.

What do we do when our thoughts defy us?
What do we do when nothing keeps its proper place?
What do we do when our thoughts take on a life of their own?

My elaborate plans for a greeting line are the first to fall in battle.

The hearty welcome. My husband is telling the thanes and their wives to sort out their own degrees. *Play the humble host.* Now he mingles with his guests whilst I sit here on the throne – alone, by myself – and wave to people in greeting, from a distance – as they seat themselves wherever they care to sit. *Pronounce it for me, sir.* I wonder whether something is the matter. *Anon, we'll drink a measure.* He speaks with two rough-looking men at the door. He will probably invite them in. I have counted out the places. It means a call for extra stools. No matter, I will stay calm and keep smiling. Chaos is always welcome when chaos comes to call. Who can those men be, I wonder? Why is my husband so silent about such undesirable friends? And why rebuff all inquiries about the Macduffs? About Banquo he is lavish in his speech. He asks me to present him eminence with both eye and tongue. He plans to open the formal events with a cheer to Banquo. I do not see Banquo here. He must be waiting to make his entrance at the sound of his name.

Scavengers killing the wounded on battlefields.
A person bleeding on the floor of a prison cell.
Straggling prisoners tied by their wrists to a horse.

It is time to set out the place-names! No, I'd rather do it myself! I will tell you what we can do! You hold the cards and follow me around the table and I will set the cards, myself, at the appropriate places! What is your name again? I know I have asked you two or three times! Simply address me as Your Majesty – that will be fine! There have been changes in the kingdom of late, as everyone is well aware, and it is important to start things off on an appropriate note! The lords and ladies will gather in the outer hall when the time arrives! Then they will be announced in the appropriate order, as they enter this room! There will be a greeting line as they enter, over there, inside the door, consisting of only a few besides your new king and your queen! They will then move on to the table and look for their places and take their seats! Then my husband and I will take our places as well! Of course there will be flourishes of the trumpets, from time to time! And the caller will announce the names as the lords and ladies enter into the room!

"You wouldn't believe the kind of tales coming out of that banquet."
"I would hate to be spreading rumours of what is not true."

Carrying out our plan - less than horrible imaginings - all i have to tell - a perfect balance - one another's throats - a body alone - the way round - ride on his back - shirk your office - upset by a little blood.

I have always been afraid to offer kindness. How to know whether a dog will bite or will lick my hand. I have lived far away from every person in my life.

The making of friendship is a gift which some people have and some do not. With you, my lord, it wasn't a case of making a friendship at all. When I met you, it was as if I was meeting myself.

The closest I came to what I take to be friendship was with Lady Macduff. I had invited her and her brood for a visit to this castle, the very day that I heard of your assault on their hearth. I looked upon her as my single friend in the kingdom at that time.

"You are generous in your offer," said one witch to another,
"But you are forgetting – for the moment – the witches' code."

I motion for the attendant to strike on the gong. *My royal lord.* Every person in the hall goes silent and turns to me. *Meeting were bare.* I stand and stretch my arms out towards my husband. As I talk, I leave the throne and take my place at the table. I call on my royal lord to give the cheer. *Good digestion wait.* Wine is poured all round and we all raise our glasses and look towards my husband. *Health on both.* I wish he would present the toast while by my side. He gives a very conciliatory pledge in favour of Banquo. *Our country's honour roofed.* It is a chance to bring the various factions together. To ease the thanes over the stile of Duncan's loss. To make them forget that foolish pledge which Duncan – in his dotage – made in favour of his inadequate son, the young and inexperienced Malcolm. Surely everyone realizes what a disastrous young king that stripling would have made. *The graced person.* We raise our glasses to drink our toast. A trick he learned of Duncan – give others praise but never give them power. Bravo, my husband, bravo. You have presented yourself as the perfect king. Kind words, well-presented, well-received. The lingering wounds of the abrupt succession have surely been healed.

Setting out the place-names.
Welcoming our guests.

The cards look quite attractive on the table! I chose the scribe whose writing I judged as the most regal hand! I sent an especially personal note to Lady Macduff! I told her that I was hoping that she would attend! I expect, I said, that we shall be especially close in future! I said I would like to count on her as my special friend! I have rooms all prepared in the palace for the couple and the children! I know that they want to be in rooms which are side by side! The Rosses and the Lennoxes here, I think, will be best! Malcolm and Donalbain here, I think, and, of course, their wives! Such a shame about Lady Banquo! Such an unfortunate trick of fate! She had crossed that stream in the spring a hundred times! Left her husband without a wife and her son without a mother! We must be especially tender with people at such stressful times!

A woman who betrays a sacred trust.

A woman whose treachery is vile.

Honours deep and broad - fog and filthy air - the length of a sword - the blooming or the withering - cure her of that - a hard hard shell - way to dusty death - threw herself away - a father teaching his son - stain spreads far and wide.

I was terrified when you began to ask about Macduff. When I heard that he had fled the kingdom I was quite relieved. You never once mentioned his lady – or their little ones.

I couldn't believe it when I heard the news. Who could conceive of doing such a thing? How many times have I chattered of Lady Macduff and her brood?

Why the Macduffs? Oh, why the Macduffs? Why the children?

"When the sun rises, it will be your future.
When the sun sets, it will be your past.
When the sun stands still, it will be your moment."

He prefers not to sit with me. *Where?* He searches for a seat among the thanes. *Which of you have done this?* What is this? – What noise is this? I raise my eyes from my regal ring and look around. *Thou cans't not say I did it.* It is my lord and he is shouting. It must be something that he sees. *Never shake thy gory locks at me.* What could possibly so upset him? Why would he scream and shake his head? This is one of those fits that plague him in the early hours.

A scribe carefully writing the words of a note.
A sleeping rider jostled on a saddle.
Two people chatting in the sunshine.

Weary se'n nights nine times nine shall he dwindle, peak and pine: though his bark cannot be lost, yet it shall be tempest-tost. Look what I have. Show me, show me. Here I have a pilot's thumb, wreck'd as homeward he did come.

A person ascending a staircase with a single candle.
A woman and a boy petting a kitten.
A balladeer strumming a lute and singing a song.

What do we do when our thoughts fly out of our control?
Are they not ours to order and command?
Does the siege of the castle take place inside the mind?

I hurry over to my lord. I command the thanes and their wives to sit.

His highness is not well. I have no idea what I am saying, but they all obey. *My lord is often thus.* I take his face in my hands. I rub his temples as I speak. *Are you a man?* I whisper as I would to a frightened child. He moves his eyes and fixes them closely on mine. *Aye, and a bold one.* He tries to search behind the irises. *That dare look on that.* He looks at me as if I am the cause of all this commotion. I try to tell him there is nothing but a stool. *The very painting of your fear.* He persists that he is seeing what he thinks he sees. *Impostors to true fear.* There was a time when he would believe whatever I say. *Make such faces?* I don't know what to tell him anymore. *When all's done.* Sir, sir, sir. *See there! Behold! Look!* You do wrong me. I am your wife. Do not forget. *How say you?* I am you and you are me. Let every other truth be banished – keep this one. He thrusts my hands away. He breaks away and strides across the room. He shouts at the empty stool. *Why, what care I?* He kicks it and it skitters across the floor. *If thou cans't nod, speak too.* He stops panting and looks around at those in the room. *Do not muse at me.* He seems to be calming down. He speaks to the gathered thanes. *I have a strange infirmity.* He calls for wine and orders another pledge.

Rescuing my husband.
Feeling need of rescue myself.

My husband, the King, told me to prepare an especial place for his good friend, Banquo! He asked me to present him eminence with both eye and tongue! Do you have his place-card there? Just shuffle until you find it! It is there for sure! I will place the great Banquo here, where my lord can easily see him as he leads the toasts! Banquo was one of the chief supports of my husband's great victory over the invaders and the rebel Scots! He will be honoured here, tonight, for his support! Oh, and do you know the name of Banquo's son? – Fleance, the card will read! Is it not next? I took extra care with his card! See?, I wrote him a little note! I said that his mother would have been proud! It is sad to think that his mother cannot be here!

A woman who lures people into her castle.
A woman who slits her guests' throats.

Counting on the good will - wolves wrangling - compatible to our depths - sprinkled into a pot - retrieve the key - that perilous stuff - losing so much sleep - the operative husk - like a stable rat - the sun is not rising.

Lady Macduff was sitting beside me. A state banquet. After one of your victories in the wars.

A toast was pledged to King Duncan. We clinked our glasses and drank his health. Then Lady Macduff turned to me and spoke of her little son.

"He asked his father, the other day, whether our family has royal blood." She set her wine glass down on the table. "I think he wants to grow up to be a king."

He went to ask advice of the three kind sisters.
"Place one pure drop of water on one small stunted flower.
This is the only way to restore the health of the land."

He raises his drink and speaks. *To our dear friend, Banquo.* He starts screaming – louder this time. *Avaunt and quit my sight!* I try to spin him around but I cannot move him. *Let the earth hide thee!* I hiss into his ear as he shouts at the overturned stool. Sir, sir, sir. *No speculation in those eyes.* Look deep into my eyes. *Take any shape but that.* Concentrate solely on me. There is nothing in this room – nothing in the world – but you and me. *Or be alive again.* We two are one. *Dare me to the desert.* This is our anchor. *The baby of a girl.* This is our rock. If ever this cable should break, we two will drift off into the mists and disappear. I reach out to rub his temples. He knocks my hands away. He will not let me touch him. He stares past my shoulder – not at me. He shouts – this time with anger. *Hence, horrible shadow!* Whatever it is, he seems to banish from his thoughts. *Unreal mockery, hence!* He stares at the stool as the thanes all stare at him.

A smithy sharpening a brace of halberds.
Witches who waylay travellers with talk of greatness.
Soldiers embedding wooden spikes in the ground.

Banquo's boy in the courtyard! The sun is a welcome respite from all that rain! Swinging a sword too big for him, but hefting it valiantly! Your father's sword, I presume? The day will come when it will seem no more than a dagger! Helping the servants to polish his armour, too, I see! A wonderful thing for a son to do! He has fought beside my husband many times! Your age, at present, my son, if you don't mind the asking? A boy like you must make his father proud! You'll be riding out with your father soon, I would wager! You'll soon have a sword and armour of your own! Very pleasant here in the sunshine! Oh, please don't rush away! I'm sure that your father is not in a hurry! I like to watch you as you work! I don't often get to talk to a boy of your age! I observe that you and your father are very close!

"There's talk about what Macbeth did and what he said he saw."
"And what Lady Macbeth did when the new king lost control."

The lion has roared - feeling need of rescue - all our yesterdays - better off alone - a perfect campaign - look everyone in the eye - under the fist - the bubbling cauldron - without my stir - the truest flight.

When I was a child, I lost a trinket. It was a little tiny ring. A tinker gave it to my mother and she gave it to me.

"This is a faery's ring," he said. "Keep it as close to you as your heart. It will always keep you safe, secure and warm."

People bury treasure and forget where they placed it. Squirrels bury nuts and starve to death. I have buried you and you have buried me.

"Mother, will I grow up to make predictions?"
She watched as her mother added a fenny snake.

I try to tell him about the mirth. *Broke the good meeting.* Where is the joy which should be the crown of this event? He looks at me as if he doesn't know me. *You make me strange.* What am I, if not your Queen? *You can behold such sights.* Do you think that I don't suffer? Do you think that I live without despair? *The natural ruby of your cheeks.* Yours only the sleepless nights? Yours only the endless hours? Do you think I look on your empty throne with a cheerful smile? Ross speaks and I am startled. All of these people – here, in our room. I shoo them out – geese in a gaggle. They shuffle and stumble out of the throne-room door. *Stones have been known.* He speaks of blood – more and more blood. *Maggot-pies, and choughs, and rooks.* How much blood has now been shed? *The secret'st blood of man.* How much more will be required? *Almost at odds with morning.* It is late. The sun will rise. We must be abed.

Winter winds
break
trees.

A woman rubbing the temples of her husband.
A bird flying north in the autumn.
A horse picking its way across a stream.

Summer breezes
nurture
flowers.

"A scorpion motif is often woven into carpets and tapestries as a means of protection from their sting."

Weather makes us
neither foolish
nor wise.

Can we threaten our thoughts with a sword?
Will they cower and slink away?

Will they find another way to take control?

He will not take his rightful place. We sit upon the floor at the foot of the empty thrones and whisper our words. *To the weird sisters.* He talks of Macduff. This has been the forbidden topic. *More shall they speak.* He has told me never to speak of Lady Macduff. But I was counting so on her presence and her support as I managed the throne. I had hoped she would be my link to the life before. *I am bent to know.* I have not seen her since the night of the Duncan deed. I need someone with whom I can spend a normal day. *In blood stepp'd in so far.* Sleep. – We both need sleep. I move from the throne to the bed to the throne without a wink – day after day. If he sleeps, he sleeps on the saddle – never at home. *Strange things have I in head.* Come sir, come sir, come. I must get my battered warrior to bed.

Chapter 13

Macbeth 7

This is the place where we met before. I can see the boiling cauldron through the mist. *Thrice the brinded cat hath mew'd.* The stench of the battlefield assails my nostrils. *Round about the cauldron go.* Putrid corpses; rusting swords; mud and blood. *Double double, toil and trouble.* Banquo, Banquo, Banquo. What did you think, my Banquo, as you were bleeding to death in the ditch? Did the witches appear and bid your gashes be closed? *In the poisoned entrails throw.* I approach them, but they do not seem to see me. Are they waiting to spring a trap? *Sweltered venom, sleeping got.* Oh, Banquo – you are the jester in the king's pack. You are the snake beneath the flower. You are the dagger which rents the fabric of my design. *Then the charm is firm and good.* The lesson of the battlefield is the lesson of the banquet. All forces – human or otherwise – respond to command. Your death – my old friend, Banquo – convinces me that predictions are challenges to act. They are busy at their potion. *How now, you secret black and midnight hags!* I take them by surprise and as they once did me.

To be the broth

A horse rearing and plunging in a mist.
A man who lives without sleeping.
A mother and her children left alone.

whose vapours cool

"The people of Scotland are no different from the people of any other land.

They want their leaders to guard their holdings, so they can sleep in their beds at night."

the fevered brain.

Who has drunk a toast with the witches?
Who has offered a pledge to their health?
Who has licked his lips at the taste of a baboon's blood?

What is this? What is this? *Speak. Demand. We'll answer.* This thunder is so loud I can hardly think. *Pour in sow's blood.* An apparition. A flash of lightning in the sky. *Eaten her nine farrow.* An armed head? Why, who else would this be but me? I am the greatest warrior that Scotland has ever known. *Beware Macduff.* One fine blow and Macduff's head shall be removed. Exactly the blow that dispatched Macdonwald. Well done! Well done! Well done! Then I shall hoist the traitor's head on a sharpened pole! *Beware the Thane of Fife.* A friendly warning from three fine friends. *Dismiss me. Enough.* All along, I have sensed that you witches are favouring me. You respect the man who can match you thought for thought.

Fine horses feeding on oats in a stall.
A young boy polishing his father's armour.
A seamstress embroidering linens.

Riding through the air! Sailing to Allepo in a sieve! Confronting a sailor's wife! Draining her husband dry as hay! Munching, as I ride, on a bag of chestnuts! Untying the winds and letting them fight against the churches! Bidding the waves to confound and swallow navigation! Making castles topple and pyramids and palaces slope their heads to their foundations! Making nature's germens tumble all together!

"King Macbeth was riding furiously through the countryside."
"His entourage was chasing him at the heels."

Speak the same language - what might have been - keeping to themselves - all life's sores - what we wish to be and do - as one weighs gold - the same shared glass - a rolled tapestry - the giving of thanks - your innermost thoughts.

I worry about you, my love. I worry about what will happen to you. I believe that there are terrible times ahead.

We have looked after each other as best we can. We each have been parent and we each have been child. I can think of no better husband nor better wife.

Our umbilical cord is now severed. We are drifting off in the dark. Your voice grows faint to me as my voice grows faint to you.

"We can read the human threads as the chapters in a book.
Perceive the unfolding of human fate in rain or in shine."

Thunder and lightning again. *Macbeth! Macbeth! Macbeth!* Another apparition against the sky. The fog opens up and a bloody child appears. This would be the child, Fleance. Soon, I will flush him out of his hiding place. I shall have the weasel's head upon a pole. *Laugh to scorn the power of man.* I always have – I always will. *None of woman born shall harm Macbeth.* I have known it all along. What do people know of witches? They do not always speak in riddles. This is plain as plain to see. The witches' task is to find for Scotland the perfect king.

Confronting the weird sisters.
Demanding to know the truth.

Arriving at the pit of Acheron! Feeling instantly at home! Conjuring up the weird sisters! Confronting them by surprise in their own liar! I have a word or two that I shall say to them! How now you secret black and midnight hags! Know that I am angry! Know that I have my reasons! Know that the wayward son was Banquo! It is he who has so held you under fortune! He loved for his own ends, not for you! Reverse those spells before I do you harm! What little you have done for me is but a mite of what you shall do! You should have included my wife in your spells! You should have called on me to take part in your conjurings! I too can show the glory of our art! I conjure up your cauldron! See it rises as I speak! Round about the cauldron sing! Elves and fairies in a ring! Four can play the magic game! Put all previous spells to shame! You must do what I shall tell! Cast a spell which will act in reverse of your previous spell!

A man whose tongue is forked like an adder.
A man who hoists his friends on sharpened pikes.

Bring her into the fold - shed his blood - fowl is fair - the horses patiently awaiting - the gathering dark - including the mind - think of water - a single candle burning - how we see ourselves - bodies stacked in rows.

Macduff is sharpening his knife. He wants England to fight his battles. His play is to cast young Malcolm aside and filch the throne.

Macduff would never make a good king. He left his wife and his babes behind – as hostages – on the battlefield. How can such a man be fit to rule this land?

If ever an arrow has hit the target it is the campaign against Macduff. He is completely unprepared for such a level of savagery. I out-bear the bear, out-lion the lion and out-tiger the tiger.

"But the sun is not rising as I stand here.
The sun is not setting as I speak.
The sun is not standing still, as we both can see."

More thunder. Louder and louder. More lightning. Blinding this time. A third apparition looms against the sky. I will ask it to tell me my future. *Listen but speak not to it.* A child with a crown on his head – a baby king. Could this be a child of mine? Could this be fortune's gift to my wife and to me? Another flash of lightning. A child with a tree in his hand – what might this be? The tree of life – but what of that? Long life to our future child. How long will our son reign as king? *Listen but speak not to it.* It speaks in a voice like thunder. *Macbeth shall never vanquished be.* I knew it all along. *Great Burnam Wood to high Dunsinane.* That will never be. *Come against him.* Come against me all and everyone. The weird sisters are on my side. There is nothing can take this crown away from me.

A group of people drinking a toast.
A boat drifting away from a dock.
Winter winds ruffling the fur of a squirrel's coat.

I myself have all the other, and the very ports they blow, all the quarters that they know i' the shipman's card. I will drain him dry as hay: sleep shall neither night nor day hang upon his pent-house lid; he shall live a man forbid.

A soldier thrusting a pike at the breast of a horse.
A prisoner being strapped into an iron chair.
A burial ground with bodies stacked in rows.

Who has swum in the waters of Acheron?
Dove deep though the waters are black?
Plunged his hand down into the muck at the bottom of Hell?

Let me tell you teasing witches a thing or two. *Make assurance double sure.* I have a design for which you have only proffered the threads. *Take a bond of fate.* I see the wall shorn of tapestry. *Tell pale-hearted fear.* I see the weavers formed-up in a line. *Sleep in spite of thunder.* The master-weaver awaiting an audience with the king. *That will never be.* Everyone thinks that you speak in riddles, but I know otherwise. *Live the lease of nature.* I don't have the gift of prophesy, but I do have the gift of knowing how best to respond. *Pay his breath to time.* You challenge me, for which I am certainly grateful. *Throbs to know one thing.* I know that you wish me to act and I shall do so. *Shall Banquo's issue ever reign in this kingdom?* There is just one more thing that I wish to know.

Viewing the apparitions.
Interpreting the signs.

Dancing about the cauldron with the witches! Double double toil and trouble! Fire burn and cauldron bubble! Round about the cauldron go! In the poison entrails throw! Throwing in a fenny snake! Throwing in my Glamis signet! Throwing in my Cawdor chain! Throwing in my Scottish crown! Throwing in my wedding ring! Cast the water of my land! Administer to a mind diseased! What you have done is not enough! Make me a father – like Banquo and Macduff! Peace I say! The charm is now wound up!

A man whose ambition is the poison which he feeds to others.
A man who sells his soul and gets nothing in return.

Feel it in your brain - battle's lost and won - this terrible deed - the love that follows - every other truth - confront the stool - the order of this realm - the crowning moment - a bulging sack - a blood-stained bundle.

So, what to say about the slaying of Lady Macduff? Of the murder of Lady Macduff and her brood? Of the slaughter of all the servants trapped in that house?

Of all his pretty ones and their dam? Of all his pretty ones and their dam at one fell swoop? Yes, my love, my orders included – all.

An old lady came to see me. She had lost her sons in the skirmishes – every one. I told her that the losing of all of all one's sons is the price one justly pays for choosing to be loyal to the losing side.

The king searched high and low.
The king searched far and wide.
Not one pure drop of water in the land.

Lightning flashes across the sky from east to west. An apparition as tall as the tallest clouds. *Show! Show! Show!* What else can you possibly show me? I am safe from harm for as long as I shall live. *Show his eyes.* Eight kings. – Why eight kings? Sons of sons of sons of my wife and me? The eighth king carries a glass. The eight becomes sixteen and then doubles again. *Grieve his heart.* Two-fold balls and treble sceptre. Will I conquer England too? Your predictions are far above any I could have devised. But what is this? – What is this? Banquo covered in blood? The self-same visage as at the banquet. Smiling at me as he did so then. Pointing at all my kings as if they belong to him. They vanish with no explanation. Come you secretive hags. What does this mean? Surely you show me what it is in my power to prevent. Otherwise why would you show such sights to a friend?

A pastry cook putting a family crest on a cake.
Travelling players putting on a show.
A man and a boy walking their horses along a path.

If I were a witch, what would I do? What would I do as I cast my thoughts around my kingdom? I would open the eyes of all those fools who insist on opposing their rightful sovereign! They would see that the warrior is always – always – the natural king! I would cleanse the minds of all who are plagued by sleeplessness, of course! I would banish all of the scorpions from the land! I would make couples whose glue is so strong that they would be forever inseparable! No summer drought nor winter storm would break them apart! And give a son to every true man of them who so wishes! And not waste sons on those who fall short in the father's part! And I would fix time – one moment in time – at Macbeth's suggestion! Not one more moment would be allowed to pass him by! If only – if only – if only I were a witch!

"They say he was searching through the fog and the mist of the battle-field."

"His soldiers warned us all to stay far away."

No thought beyond a smile - the best that is in us - launch myself into the air - where am I now - heart would fain deny - a neighbour's talk - the perfect fusion of minds - cannot be good - no human being - lost in a mist or a fog.

I've taken to sleeping on the floor at the foot of my throne. A sword and a dagger in my hands. I trust no guards because guards will sleep and snore.

I have no friends and wish to have none. I prefer my enemies ranged around me in the dark. I can see their eyes and their claws in the campfire's glow.

I have lowered the action to a level that has left them paralyzed. Don't challenge Macbeth unless you are a Macbeth. Blood for blood, tooth for tooth, nail for nail.

"Mother, will I make riddles which can't be solved?"
She watched as her mother added a baboon's blood.

The fog rolls over the battlefield. The stench of the corpses is all I can bear. *Ay sir, all this is so.* Know, noble Banquo, that I will find that son of yours – though he be hiding in a weasel's hole – and do for him what I have done for you. *The best of our delights.* The witches stir their cauldron. *Why stands Mac-*

beth so amazedly? I will make you a prediction, my noble Banquo. I shall have it chiselled on your tombstone. Banquo – The Plaything of the Three Weird Sisters. Dead Father to a Line of Uncrowned Kings. *His welcome pay.* The witches reappear and disappear. *Perform your antick round.* Banquo, Banquo, Banquo. You have seen what it can be to rely on these juggling witches. You were foolish enough to believe they were favouring you. Did it ever occur to you that they were seeking your response to what they were saying? That your future was in your hands – not in theirs? Our destiny, my Banquo, is not in the seeds that the witches offer, but in those which we choose to crush or choose to plant. *Come like shadows, so depart.* In the distance I hear the galloping of horse. *Come in, without there!* Your king craves news of what is happening in his land.

If water was ice
thought the bird in summer,
I would never drown.

A sleeper tossing and turning on a floor.
An armour-bearer sharpening a sword.
A ring at the bottom of a cauldron.

If ice was water
thought the bird in winter,
I would never freeze.

"All known scorpion species possess venom and use it primarily to kill or paralyse their prey."

The bird flew
north in the autumn
and south in the spring.

Can one come back from one's darkest actions?
Is there a pathway which leads upward from that pit?
What is the price of such a ticket if one were for sale?

So Macduff has fled to England, has he? Well I am nothing if not a man who learns from the past. I acted too late in response to the predictions concerning Banquo. I see now that these three weird sisters were testing my mettle. These words about Macduff are not a prediction, but rather a test. They are designed to sound the depths of Macbeth as a king. Macduff, Macduff, Macduff. *The very firstlings of my heart.* I am not the weird sisters, who offer riddles bated with cheese. *The very firstlings of my head.* I am the one who knows your most vulnerable weaknesses. *The castle of Macduff I will surprise.*

I am the snake who stalks your child in your flowerbed. *Give to the edge of the sword.* I shall reach inside your chest and remove your heart. *His wife, his babes and all unfortunate souls.* The witches are lost in the mists. Their chanting has faded away. They leave behind the putrid stench of the battlefield.

Chapter 14

Lady Macbeth 7

The castle of Lady Macduff. Meeting my husband's associates in the hall. Who did bid me join you? Why my husband, Macbeth, of course. He has a spy in every castle. Everyone who is loyal to him has a spy in his midst. I am here to oversee your work today. He enjoins you to follow the plan to the final letter. Leave no rubs nor botches, please, in the work. I shall keep my own hands clean. I am merely here to observe. I represent my husband in every respect.

To be the laughter

Sunlight streaming through the bars of a portcullis.
A woman sitting and chatting with her children.
Guards smiling and chatting as they open a gate.

which echoes cheerfully

"The people of Scotland are no different from the people of any other land.
They want a man of God to tell them the right and the wrong."

through the halls.

Who has been whipped for doing a kindness?
Who has been scourged for thinking kind thoughts?
Who has sacrificed for a neighbour and paid the cost?

Lady Macduff is chatting with Ross. *School yourself.* I do not know Ross any more. *Fits of the season.* I should have asked my husband whether Ross is still loyal to our cause. *We are traitors.* Nothing he says reveals his allegiance. *Do not know ourselves.* He is trying to save her life and that of her children. *What they were before.* But not, it would seem, if it means the expense of his own. *Blessing upon you.* Save yourself, he says, and I will do the same.

A horseman hacking furiously with a battle sword.
Predictions which cause confusion in the realm.
A soldier slitting a throat with his dagger.

Today I am Lady Macduff! In a chamber in my castle! Bantering away the time with our little boy! Chiding one another of many, many things! Of ravens and hawks and mousing owls! Of fathers who run away! Of traitors and liars and swearers! Of kings and fools! Such a cheerful little chatterer! The only boy on earth who would speak to a parent like this! Too young for his father's armour! He disappears inside the helm! He tried to lift the sword and broke my vase! Well, chatter on my boy – your time will come as sure as the sunrise! You are not just another boy, oh no – you are your father and mother's son! Your father is preparing a place for you at the top of the hill!

"She must have known what went on inside that castle."
"Everyone says the two of them are as thick as thieves."

No exceptions allowed - the night-watch napping - the inauguration of the tranquillity - don't come back - the greater half of me - their proper place - just enough light - two elements fighting - what was a riddle - swallowing the bait.

I miss laughter and cheerful children. A group of old friends with mulled wine by a winter fire. All of that ceased when the banquet broke up that night.

The old dog is my only companion. And he is not long for this world. He has slept through events that have made my blood run cold.

Why ask forgiveness or try to change things? It is how we are seen – not how we see ourselves. Turn around on your horse and you'll find he still goes the same way.

"But no witch is permitted to witness the blooming or the withering
Of her own or another witch's seeds of time."

The lady chatters with her son. *Your father's dead.* I could listen to this for hours. *What will you do now?* Stay your hands awhile, while I listen to this pleasing rapport. *How will you live?* The two or them together are every mother's ideal of a mother and her son. *Yes, he is dead.* Is the boy loyal to his father? Are you noticing what he says? Do any of you have family at home? *How will you do for a husband?* Keep your hands away from your knives, there is plenty of time. *Was my father a traitor, mother?* You will have blood aplenty before the day is through.

Spying in the lady's castle.
Becoming Lady Macduff.

Bantering with my protector! On good days you are my protector, but not on bad? You come to warn me of danger, and then run away? Where is my husband, you silly fool? Why has he not come with you? If there were danger, he would certainly be here! Oh, the things that you do not know! My husband and I are thick and fast! We never, never leave each other's side! Go and look around the corner and he will be there! You have no idea what he would go through to protect me! And you have no idea what I would do for him! My husband and I are two-as-one! – One-as-two! Go on and save your petty little existence for what it's worth to you! Run away and hide for the rest of your measly life! My son and I will face these ruffians alone!

A woman who betrays her fellow women.
A woman who delights in the slaughter of children.

A diver touching the bottom - a life of their own - catch this updraught - yoked together - to the last syllable - angel on the left - cheapest thing for sale - gold for information - a warrior's deed - requested a minor change.

I heard laughter in the kitchen the other day. The two pastry-cooks froze and stood with their faces dabbed in flour. They were petrified that it would be off with their heads.

I offered to help the girl who churns the butter in the courtyard outside the creamery. Her hands were trembling as she tried to show me how it was done. Then her eye started to twitch and so I thanked her and then I turned and walked away.

We lost the man who tastes our food. He disappeared sometime in the night. I never told you that I took over that role myself.

"You are wrong about the sun not rising.
You are wrong about the sun not setting.
You are wrong about the sun not standing still."

Stay your hands a little longer. Sheath your knives and wait for a moment. *Bless you fair dame.* You are too eager to practice your craft. *Your state of honour.* Let this messenger approach. *Danger does approach.* Let us hear what Lady Macduff – in response – will say. *Be not found here.* A final chance, perhaps, to gather up her brood and fly away. *With your little ones.* Has she no secret doorways leading to secret chambers? *I am too savage.* Has her husband not provided such basic defence? *Were fell cruelty.* And why did her husband not take the lady and their children with him? *Too nigh your person.* What kind of man would leave his wife completely alone? *Heaven preserve you.* The messenger turns and leaves. *I dare abide no further.* His plan, it appears, is only to save himself. The guards who we left in the courtyard will alter that plan.

A girl mixing butter in a churn.
A cook stirring a pot in a scullery.
A group of men with daggers at their sides.

Her husband's to Aleppo gone, master o' the Tiger: but in a sieve I'll thither sail, and, like a rat without a tail, I'll do, I'll do, and I'll do. I'll give thee a wind. Thou'rt kind. And I another.

A porter answering a knock in the morning.
A man and a woman admiring a tapestry.
A warrior trying the heft of a new sword.

Who has forced the door of his neighbour?
Who has stretched him on a rack?
Who has squeezed every bubble of blood from his anguished frame?

You may now approach my lady – but only approach. Her face is calm for all her fear. *Whither should I fly?* She hugs her son and holds him closely. *I remember now.* What mother in the kingdom would not do the same? *In this earthly world.* She is acting as if at court. *To do harm.* She is presenting a lucid defence. *To do good.* Save your breath, my lady. – The courts of compassion are not operative here. *Dangerous folly.* Here your only recourse is to take down one of those antique broadswords from the wall and let that be your reason for staying alive. *Done no harm.* You look to me for a signal. I can see you are tired of waiting. Well, your wait is at an end. Unsheathe your daggers now, for your time has come.

Fighting fiercely for my son.
Succumbing to the murderers' blows.

The uncouth ruffians enter the chamber! They are not a surprise to me! I saw them enter into the courtyard down below! They are demanding to see my husband! My husband is not for you! If he were here he would unseam you all with one swift blow! Our boy stands up and defies them! I must protect our boy! I stand up and move towards them! You know not what you do! The daggers fall like rain! I raise my arms to protect our boy! He is all my husband has! He will reign someday in this kingdom! The rain of blows is relentless! You are trampling the seed of our future! Oh bludgeon me as you will, but spare the boy!

A woman who thirsts after blood.
A woman whose spell is like a witch.

Riddles which can't be solved - the great restorative - no heavenly protection - gavel of judgment - fair is fowl - drift up to the heavens - cuts off a hand - not loud but deep - the stories of all the souls - down into the muck.

The wardrobe-lady's little girl was bright and cheerful with me the other day. I came across her as she entertained her dolls. So obvious – I kept thinking – that she doesn't know who I am.

I see fear in the eyes of the little children. I see it when we ride through the market square. Their parents have taught them all to stand still and not laugh or say a word.

Whatever happened to those travelling players? I kept assuring you that I was sure they meant no harm. They had no idea why you grew so angry all at once.

All the water in the land was brackish, bitter and foul.
Beside the king the princess was silently crying.
She was crying because the peasants had nothing to drink.

The boy is fiercely defiant. A wren against an owl. A mouse against a hawk. His greatest desire is to protect his mother. Her greatest desire is protection of him. The two will share their fate together until the end. This is the Scotland of the Macbeths. Crime is innocence and innocence is crime. The knife is plunged into the boy as deep as the heart.

A helmet filled with blood on the battlefield.
Spikes biting deep into human flesh.
A captain swinging a battle axe with all his might.

Lady Macduff's young son! In the throne room, before the coronation! Hello young boy, do not be frightened! You are the son of Lady Macduff – I remember you well! You are the boy who brought the cage with the fine-plumed birds! I saw you ride beneath our battlements as you arrived! I see your little kitten has run away! You get on one side of the throne and I will place myself on the other! Together we will catch the little scamp! Oh, I see it covets the throne! Not alone in that regard, I am bound to say! Where are your mother and your father? Last minute readiness, no doubt! I have been dressed for it seems like hours! My husband is nowhere to be found! How its little heart is beating! Does your kitten have a name? Please stay a little longer! Surely your parents wouldn't begrudge! They will blow the trumpets long before the start!

"There are rumours that the two Macbeths were present."
"Some say the two of them did this terrible deed themselves."

Devoid of hope - win us to our harm - a prancing steed - never be swept away - two buckets in a well - we are your guest - the innocent flower - cannot be ill - scorpion mating ritual - imagine the magnificent pageant.

I don't know when I am in touch with my deepest thoughts. When I am awake – do you think – or when I am asleep? I don't know whether it is waking or sleeping that I fear the most.

Do you know the boy who fetches the firewood? He brought the hatchet into the hall the other day. I sat with my back to him – waiting for it all to end.

I often walk upon the battlements. I lean over the parapet. I watch the activity in the courtyard down below.

"Will I grow up to snare souls and topple kingdoms?"
She watched as her mother stirred the bubbling cauldron.

Lady Macduff is running away. Before they can turn to her, she rushes across the room. She plunges through the doorway and runs down the hall. Her screams are for her children. She calls to the nurses to lock the door. I have no wish to follow her struggles. I can hear them from where I am standing, here in the chamber. The man who she married is off to England. The man who I married is not here today. He is planning similar scenes all over the kingdom. As she screams, I place my hands over both my ears.

An arrow
fell from the sky
and killed a man.

A lady explaining that she and her children are innocent.
Nurses reading stories to girls and boys.
A pool of blood coagulating on the flagstones.

"An arrow
cannot fall from the sky,"
a wise man averred.

"The speed of the scorpion's venom is faster, many say, than a lightning strike."

Such wisdom
has never brought anyone
back to life.

Who has spilled the blood on the flagstones?
Who has knelt to clean it up?
Which has been the more efficient of the two?

This castle is like a battlefield. There is blood all over the floor. Here, where the lady struggled to save her son. Here, where the boy was caught and silenced for good. Here, where the other children were found in their nursery. All credit to their nurses, for staying loyal to their last breath. Here in the scullery, the pot is still boiling over the fire. Here in the courtyard, the guards are lying as if they have fallen asleep at their posts. Decay will soon set in. Nature's laws are never denied. Soon the castle will reek of the stench of those who laughed and bantered and giggled. Pile the bodies in the courtyard. Leave the castle as clean as you can. Will the smoke drift up to the heavens or fade away? You have served your master well. I shall give you an excellent report. Did you say you had family at all? Your work is done for the day. You may now go home.

Chapter 15

Macbeth 8

So the thanes all fly away. *Bring me no more reports.* Better weather, I presume, in England. *Let them fly all.* Better that all these scurrilous traitors should run away. *I cannot taint with fear.* Better to have all my enemies ranged against me than to have half of them entering battle at my back. *What's the boy Malcolm?* One decisive battle – that is all I shall need. *Till Birnham wood remove.* One decisive battle against these traitors and their English cohorts and everything will become what I want it to be. *No man that's born of woman.* I am a man who stands on a rock. *The mind I sway by.* The shifting sands of petty reports have no effect on my position. *The heart I bear.* If I am Scotland, and Scotland is I, what need I fear?

To be the armour

A scorpion slowly moving over a surface.
Flowers tossing and turning in the breeze.
A curiosity exhibited on a stage.

which resists all assaults

"The people of Scotland are no different from the people of any other land.
They want for their old folks to sit by the fire and tell the old stories."

against body and brain.

Is one man shackled to a wall while other men talk of their children?
Do torn fingernails lead to the telling of purer truths?
Does the torturer eat his lunch without leaving the room?

There is nothing in this for myself. *Sick at heart.* Everything that I do is for Scotland alone. *Lived long enough.* This coming battle is not designed to bring honour to me. *My way of life.* I need nothing for myself. *Fallen into the sere.* I have barely sat on the throne since I have been king. *Honour, love, obedience.* I have left the greater half of me behind. *Troops of friends.* I have remade myself for Scotland. *Curses, not loud but deep.* I have exchanged the milk of human kindness for bitter resolve. *Mouth-honour, breath.* I have hollowed myself to the core. *Poor heart would fain deny.* I have retained nothing of Macbeth but the operative husk.

An old dog asleep beneath a table.
A lady's horse stepping gingerly into a stream.
A family walking to market with baskets of vegetables.

I am a scorpion! I am trying not to think! I am trying simply to be what I am meant to be! I move like a warrior against my enemy! I enter into his brain! I move over the surface, stinging as I go! I enrage him to destruction! I make a scorpion of the man whose brain I sting!

"There are very strange rumours coming out of that castle."
"I hear that the servants are fleeing Dunsinane."

Such a small atom - a frightened child - owe him nothing - keep in mind our pledge - a horse sinking slowly - a whimsical dream - must not look to have - your hoped-for self - a desolate landscape - the puddles on my path.

Let me tell you about my day, my love. It is not what I expected my life to be. Not what I once saw as the routine agenda of a king.

I attend hangings. Sometimes a dozen a day. I supervise the raising of heads on pikes.

Even boys who cross the line. There was a lad the other day. I gave the nod and had him put away.

"I have drunk the blood of humans; I have drunk the blood of baboons;
But a witch's blood I am wise enough to decline."

And the Queen, Doctor? – What of the Queen? *Not so sick.* The mind is merely an agent of the will. *Troubled with thick-coming fancies.* I have carved my way through formations as thick as hewn oak. *Keep her from her rest.* I have made carnage of the ranks of veteran armies. *Minister to a mind diseased.* I have taken the cream of military might and left it torn and bleeding in the mud. *Pluck from the memory.* There is nothing that one can put in front of me – including the mind – including the mind – which I cannot design a method by which to scale. *Raze out the written troubles.* There is no castle which is impregnable. – No castle wall which can never be breached. *Cleanse the stuff'd bosom.* There is no castle in the world which cannot fall.

Hanging all the traitors.
Spying on my thanes.

I sense that I am not alone! I scan the battlefield from left to right! From where I crawl to the horizon! To the east and to the west! An army of moving scorpions! Crawling across the landscape! Stinging as they go! Striking terror into the host on which they ride!

A man whose servants tremble with fear whenever he calls.
A man whose friends are all dead or escaped abroad.

I remember very little - the routine agenda - languishing in a cell - nerves and doubts and fears - my elaborate plans - the bottom of hell - creeps in this petty pace - taking each other's measure - under heavy judgement - merge your mind.

The clock makes a sound like a booming drum. The fire crackles like a thunderstorm. My eyes feel like they are bleeding and my eardrums ache.

There was a crowned scarecrow in a hangman's noose on the hillside. As I rode near Dunsinane. I was too bone-weary to order a scourge of the countryside.

I don't look forward to seeing the sun rise. I don't rejoice as the sun goes down. The blackest night with the fewest stars is what pleases me now.

An old man and a boy stood on a hillside.
It is not known which was the first to speak.

I am surrounded by fools and incompetents. *Devil damn thee black.* These reports that they bring me are false. *Cream-face loon.* I know what I want to hear when I send out for news. *Geese, villain?* These fools have not heard the witches. *Lily-livered boy.* They do not know the rock on which I stand. *What soldiers, patch?* Once I hang them all, the cause will be better served. *What soldiers, whey-face?* I will not hear of foreign soldiers with a foot on Scottish soil. I will not hear of Scottish thanes going over to the enemy. *Hang those that talk of fear.* I will not hear talk of defeat on the eve of a victory. I want to control not just what I see but what I am told.

A king rising to start his daily routine.
A man taking a drink from a river of blood.
A father teaching his son to hunt with a falcon.

I come, Graymalkin! Paddock calls. Anon. Fair is foul, and foul is fair: hover through the fog and filthy air. Where hast thou been, sister? Killing swine. Sister, where thou? A sailor's wife had chestnuts in her lap, and munch'd, and munch'd, and munch'd:– 'Give me,' quoth i: 'Aroint thee, witch!' the rump-fed ronyon cries.

Crushed helmets and rusting swords on a battlefield.
Letters which are written in the recipient's blood.
A starving rat chewing the guts of a living man.

If we break another's bones have we broken a trust?
If we pluck out another's eyes do we lose our sight?
Can we learn his secrets without revealing our own?

What have I become? *I'll fight.* I am Macbeth – not Duncan, nor Banquo, nor Macduff. *My flesh be hacked.* They say that the ancient warriors used to eat the heart of a warrior whom they had defeated. Why would anyone eat the heart of a coward or a fool? *Send out more horses.* Is there something that makes us become what we overcome? When we climb a hill do we leave our best selves on the trail? *Skirr the country round.* There have always been two Macbeths. My wife was the first to see this. She sat me beside the fire and told me of me. *Give me mine armour.* That I had greatness and I had weakness and the two were closely commingled. She told me that she could only love the one. *Give me mine armour.* Well, all is settled now. The mousing-owl has become the hawk. I see the gleaming of my breast-plate in her eyes. The castle which I have conquered is the mind of Macbeth.

Preparing for the battle.
Thinking about my wife.

I am one of you! I am one of you! I think no thoughts! I show no mercy! I make everyone my victims! I need no one to share my feelings! I have no feelings to share! I am a scorpion and a scorpion lives alone among other scorpions! Scorpions live and die by the rules of the scorpions' code! And when I die I will turn to dust and blow in the winds away! No porter at the gates of a scorpion heaven or hell!

A man who cripples those who bring him unwelcome news.
A man whose parents would disown him if they were alive.

Their tongues cut out - the other angel - just out of sight - as if i am the cause - meet with macbeth - the rain of blows - hands over both my ears - mule who delivers - their blood-soaked armour - yield to that suggestion.

I keep myself busy hearing reports from all my spies. I have a spy in every house throughout the land. I even have spies in England – just to be sure.

I have spies who report to spies who report to me. I have spies who spy on the spies who spy on the spies. You, my love – and I – are the only two humans on earth whom I never doubt.

I only have one item in my plans. It is to unseam Macduff from the nave to the chaps. Beyond that, I have no further plans.

The king collected a teardrop from the tear-duct of the princess.
He placed that teardrop on the leaf of one stunted flower.
That teardrop brought abundance back to the land.

The day will come. – I know the day will come. *Throw physic to the dogs.* The day will come when there will be no more sleepless nights. *Cast the water of my land.* My wife will hold a banquet, and everyone will come. *Find her disease.* There will be toasts for all and sundry. *Purgative drug.* Plenty to drink and plenty to eat. And stories of the times when we all were young. *Therein the patient must minister to himself.* And Scotland shall be strong, with all her enemies safely at bay. And everyone there will look everyone in the eye.

A monk chanting prayers in a cell.
An old lady under a blanket beside a fire.
A charwoman with chaffed elbows scrubbing flagstones.

Why could I not have a son? Why should Banquo be favoured with a son and then with the crown for all time to come? Suppose that Banquo had been the barren one? What then would the witches have said? Would they have made him king for the interim and then predicted that Macbeth's issue – the boy who stood beside me – would later be king? Witches – hear me now! I call out to you in the wilderness! If my boy had been beside me, I know what you would have predicted! All hail Macbeth! Thine issue shall reign in this kingdom! All hail Macbeth! Thou shalt get kings though thou be none! All hail Macbeth! Your children shall be kings!

"Many of the thanes are going over to side with Malcolm."
"No human being could do what was done to the Macduffs."

I see the patterns - a miniature kingdom - urges her husband - the bottom of a well - as deep as to the heart - the murk of life - knock at my ribs - blooming in the field - slowly bleeding away - the deed is the deed.

Do we forge pathways through the murk of life? Or does life itself direct us to certain paths? What determines where each footstep eventually falls?

I determined that I would always look straight ahead. Whatever the meadow or thicket which lay in my path. To be the captain who never deviates from the course.

Some swim in pristine streams. Some swim in rivers of blood. Each is trying to get to the other side.

"Don't talk to me while I am working," said the mother.
"I snared two souls and toppled a kingdom by mistake."

And what of the Queen? How does the Queen of Scotland on this day? *The Queen, my lord, is dead.* So this is your report? *She should have died hereafter.* There was a day when we walked in a meadow. *There would have been a time.* We rode our horses to get to that place, so it was one or two hours ride from the castle. *Tomorrow, and tomorrow, and tomorrow.* The innocent flowers were tossing and turning in the breeze that came down from the hillside. *All our yesterdays.* We walked and talked, hand in hand, for an hour or two. *Out, out, brief candle!* Lately, I have taken that ride alone – east, west, north, south – and I have never found that meadow. *A tale told by an idiot.* I shall never look for that meadow, ever again.

A seeker
climbed
a mountain.

The head of a swimmer breaking the surface.
An eye seeking an entrance to the mind.
A person putting another person on display.

Seeking
wisdom
at the top.

"The venom of the scorpion is also used as a defence against what it perceives to be a dangerous predator."

The view
from the mountaintop
was all he found.

Does the torturer hate his victims and love his horse?
Does the torturer pause to give his kitten some milk?
Does the torturer teach his boy the lore of his trade?

No reports – I said no more reports. *The wood began to move.* Well, the witches give and the witches take away. *You may see it coming.* This is the rule of life. *If thou speak'st false.* Now the tide rolls in and now the tide rolls out. *Doubt the equivocation.* Duncan, Banquo, Macduff – they were not alive to life. They did not hear the crickets cry and the owl call. They were not aware of the serpent under the flower. *Lies like truth.* Birnham Wood is another challenge. – Born of woman is my touchstone. *A weary of the sun.* The tide rolls out and the tide rolls in. *The estate o'the world.* The witches have taken me on as their champion. I must not let them down. *Blow wind, come wrack.* I shall never be defeated until the witches are proven wrong. *Harness on our back.* If their promise fails, then they are failures too.

Chapter 16

Lady Macbeth 8

I don't believe that I am sleepwalking. The gentlewoman says that I do, but I don't believe her. The doctor, too, reports that I walk in my sleep, but my husband says that the doctor is deficient in expertise. Each day, I have such a long watch that I am exhausted completely. I have the running of the entire castle with which to contend. I am the lady of the house, with obligations which I am duty-bound to perform. I patrol the halls and check on the servants. I help them to set out the place-names. I explain the protocol for the official banquets and inform them of who, this night, will be our especial guest. I ask the servants for their reports. I ask them whether they noticed the boy, Fleance, at his mother's funeral. I ask them whether they observed Lady Macduff at the coronation of myself and my lord. I ask them whether Banquo is gone from the court. I ask them where, do they think, my husband might possibly be. At night, I lie down on my pillow, in the chamber next the throne, and fall into as deep a sleep as any servant girl who sighs and sinks down, exhausted, into the hay.

To be the sleep

Moonlight shining on the courtyard of a castle.
A single candle glowing at the end of a corridor.
A lone figure shuffling in the dark.

which closes the eyes

"The people of Scotland are no different from the people of any other land.

When things go wrong in Scotland, the people will not forbear."

and rests the mind.

Is love a sunny meadow?
Is love a foggy rain-soaked trail?
Is love a sudden opening in the earth?

The gentlewoman reports to the doctor. *Rise from her bed.* The gentlewoman reports to my husband. *Her nightgown on.* The gentlewoman reports to me whenever I question her as to her duties. *Afterwards seal it.* She says that I walk at night. – I deny the same. *Not report after her.* Why would I walk at night, I ask, when I can easily walk in the day? *Light by her continually.* Why would I talk to myself, I ask, when I can easily talk to you? *Washing her hands.* When I can easily talk to the doctor? *Spoke what she should not.* When I can easily talk to my husband? *Such a heart in my bosom.* Why would I walk at night, when I would be sure to do my royal person harm?

Mousing owls attacking soaring hawks.
A person feeling himself slowly bleeding to death.
Thoroughbred horses smashing the sides of their stalls.

I am standing on the castle wall! Studying curiously the great commotion down below! Intense activity in the courtyard! The conquered and the conqueror! Breastplates glistening in the sun! The kneeling of deference! The bow of acknowledgment! The passing of tribute from servant to servant down the line! The horses patiently awaiting their bags of oats!

"Macbeth is nothing but a butcher."
"Lady Macbeth is his fiend-like queen."

Seen inside my dream - only one leg - washing the mind - honour, love, obedience - would i save myself - have grown stronger - plan is so simple - give the witches legitimacy - a mind brim-full - what they will see.

I used to watch the ladies weaving the tapestry. The overseer, you recall, was a prickly old man. As the project went on, he grew tired of my concerns.

Perhaps it is women's way. Perhaps the prerogative of the Queen. But I would bring him a new idea almost every day.

I would watch the weavers weaving. Watch the various-coloured threads as they wove their way to and fro in this vast design. And they would put their work aside at the end of the day.

A witch was alone on a desolate wayside.
She stopped a warrior who was dressed in battle array.

Yet here's a spot. Out, damned spot! out, I say! – One: two: why, then, 'tis time to do't. – Hell is murky! – Fie, my lord, fie! a soldier, and afeard? What need we fear who knows it, when none can call our power to account? – Yet who would have thought the old man to have had so much blood in him.

Spying on the gentlewoman.
Spying on the doctor.

I am standing on the battlements! The ceremony goes on! The passing of deference and allegiance from hand to hand! My child is a blood-stained bundle! He lies in the courtyard for all to see, but no one acknowledges him! Blood is seeping from his wrappings! The bloody stain spreads far and wide! The parley of rights and duties continues on!

A woman who strikes with fang and claw.
A woman who drinks her victim's blood.

You must allay all fears - what was known - there are rumours - the warmth of the sun - upon the heath - to snare souls - tugging at its tether - chaos comes to call - as clearly as i see you - such a level of savagery.

And the next day, I would ask the master-weaver if he would indulge me if I requested a minor change in the design. I'd had a chance to sleep on it, you might say. I had thought about what it was that I wanted our new tapestry to portray.

Should it end with the day we were wed? Should it end with the day we met? Should most of it be concerned with the days of our youth?

The master-weaver would throw up his hands. "Madame, I realize that you are the Queen. But are you the master-weaver here or am I?"

A lady thought she knew her husband well.
A husband thought he knew his lady well.

The doctor watches me. *No truth in your report.* He tells me that he has been asked to do so by my husband. *Great perturbation in nature.* My husband tells me that all this watching is for my good. *Slumbery agitation.* I tell my husband that there is no need. *Heard her say?* I tell the doctor that I never walk in my sleep. *Came she by that light?* I walk the halls late at night because the day is too short to perform the duties of a queen. *Her eyes are open.* Doctor, tell me truly, if I were sound asleep, would I carry a lighted candle? *She rubs her hands.* How could a candle possibly offer light to closed eyes? *Satisfy my remembrance.* Doctor, if I may tell you truly, you are no more the master of your profession than the least of my lowliest maids. *Known what you should not.* My maids have failed me time and again. *Heart is sorely charged.* My maids have left me on my own to fetch and carry. *Beyond my practice.* They fail to provide sufficient water for the washing of my hands.

A gentlewoman whispering to a doctor.
Two people sitting and watching in the dark.
A lady who is constantly washing her hands.

When shall we three meet again in thunder, lightning, or in rain? When the hurlyburly's done, when the battle's lost and won. That will be ere the set of sun. Where the place? Upon the heath. There to meet with Macbeth.

A pot of stew bubbling over a fire.
A mason pointing-up a crack in a wall.
A tinker sharpening knives on an emery wheel.

Is love a letter written in ink?
Is love a letter written in blood?
Is love a letter written in a language which we cannot read?

The thane of Fife had a wife: where is she now? – What, will these hands ne'er be clean?– No more o' that, my lord, no more o' that: you mar all with this starting. Here's the smell of the blood still: all the perfumes of Arabia will not sweeten this little hand. Oh, oh, oh!

Spying on my husband.
Spying on myself.

I am standing on the parapet! I grasp the stones with my toes! I launch myself into the air above the crowd! I float above the bustling courtyard! I float above my blood-soaked babe! I float above the conquerors and the conquered! The sunlight gleams on their blood-soaked armour! I cannot tell which is which from this great height! If I let myself fall from the air, I shall dash my brains out!

A woman who has no human feelings.
A woman who hisses like a fiend.

What he can see - thinking for two - the balance of my crown - would have been a time - what has worked so well - day's worst work - hollowed myself to the core - alter that plan - begging for pennies - my boyhood fits.

We were riding through a muddy market town. I have never been good at remembering names. The town was small, and the market was not robust.

A crowd had gathered – as is always the case in these towns – to watch the royal progress. I could feel the drizzle run down the back of my neck. I was holding, with one hand, the reins of my horse, and with the other hand, I was trying to right the balance of my crown.

And there was a lady in the crowd. She was standing amidst her brood. Rain and drizzle not withstanding – she was a queen.

A person was sure that he could solve a riddle.
It seemed logical to start from what is known.

My husband is always in the field. *How does your patient doctor?* He is preparing for a glorious battle. *Thick-coming fancies.* He is always scurrying round the countryside. *Keep her from her rest.* He leaves the gentlewoman and the doctor by my side. *A mind diseased.* He asks the doctor to banish my troubles. *A rooted sorrow.* The doctor says that he cannot comply. *Raze out the written troubles.* I tell the both of them that I am not in need of help. *Sweet oblivious antidote.* I need no gentlewomen, nor doctors, nor antidotes. *Minister to himself.* I only need my husband by my side.

A ghost appearing at a formal banquet.
A torturer turning a screw with a steady hand.
A single candle lighting a murderer's way.

A babe like no other! I love to hold you at my breast! A son to please his father! Growing up by leaps and bounds! A warrior's form already! My back is sore from carrying you around! Your father sleeps like a baby since you have been born! A load off weary shoulders! The succession is now assured! I have hardly slept a wink since my laying-in – no I have not! A lot you care, as long as you have your accustomed milk! You are drinking me, you snug little fellow; drinking me and all I am! Too precious to pass you on to the nursing maids! You shall be your mother's child as well as your father's! You shall be the best of your father and mother both! Take your time – I can stay up all night! Drink as deep as your father drinks! We must nurse you into manhood! A stately princeling of the realm! Some day, my boy, you shall wear your father's crown!

"Better the both of them should be dead than rule in this kingdom."
"Many say that they will not be long for this world."

No drawback in the exercise - one small stunted flower - the best of the men - welcome in your eye - suffered an injury - my seeds alone - snuffs out lives - thicken my carapace - look for that meadow - best not think at all.

And I had a notion – just for a moment – that I should stop the royal train, and climb down into the mud, and put my crown upon this lady, and sweep my robe around her shoulders, and bid the footmen help her to mount my horse, and let this lady take my place as Scotland's Queen.

And what of me? What would I do? Would I take this lady's place among her brood?

But I knew. I knew in the midst of this fantasy – queen or not? That there could never be another place for me.

A group of witches made up riddles by the dozens.
They posed a riddle to everyone they met.

Wash your hands, put on your nightgown; look not so pale. – I tell you yet again, Banquo's buried; he cannot come out on's grave. To bed, to bed! there's knocking at the gate: come, come, come, come, give me your hand. What's done cannot be undone. – To bed, to bed, to bed!

Rock and water
are
hammer and tong.

A candle flickering, almost dying, and flickering again.
Whispered voices echoing faintly in the halls.
A figure turning and shuffling slowly away in the dark.

Choose to be rock
if time
is your foe.

"The scorpion's venom is a mixture of compounds, each not only causing a different effect but also designed to paralyse a specific prey."

Choose to be water
if time
is your friend.

What is love if it comes with a stinger?
What is love if we fear to drown?
What is love if we fail to reach the other side?

They are all afraid that I shall commit suicide. That is why the doctor and the gentlewoman keep constant watch. There are dozens of other spies whom my husband keeps in pay. He tells me that all are employed to keep me safe. On the contrary, I say, I shall probably live forever. I shall be Queen of the Kingdom of Scotland for all of time. Is that not the fate in the adage? The one the children tell when they are let to stay up late and tell hair-curling stories around the fire? You will get your wish of the moment and then you will be condemned to live that wish on earth – every second, every minute, every hour, every day – until the end of time. I will sit on my throne, in my empty room, and think my thoughts. Thoughts that lead to nothing but more thoughts and more thoughts and more thoughts. If only my husband would sit beside me from time to time.

Chapter 17

Macbeth 9

I spy Macduff through the smoke and the mist. *Tyrant show thy face.* Well this is the moment I have been seeking. – Face to face with the one who deserted his wife and his brood. *My wife and children's ghosts.* Shouting his wrath to the heavens. Turn, my friend, and speak your words to me. *My sword with an unbattered edge.* You have proven yourself inferior. You left your brood and fled to another country, my friend. *One of greatest note.* Which of us lacks the kingly attributes? Which is fit to rule the land? *Let me find him, fortune!* If I had a son, would I save myself and leave my boy behind?

To be the sword

A horse plodding along in a well-worn rut.
A warrior fatigued from a high-pitched battle.
Figures looming ahead in the fog and the rain.

which brings these events

"The people of Scotland are no different from the people of any other land.
They want all things set to rights or they want to know why."

to a welcome close.

Who can say I led life gently?
Found it pastures of greenest grass?
Fashioned an enclave against the night and the hungry wolves?

I carve my way across the battle field. Young Siward falls by my sword. His father's son, though just a boy. I see the English are not true-born fighters. The wretched kerns fall one by one. *Play the Roman fool.* I know who my target is. Your death will not be on my conscience. – You and I are two of a kind. Had I not murdered Duncan you – you, my friend – would be sure to have done so. I would not have had the crown for long before I felt your dagger in my ribs. *Die on mine own sword.* I could see it in your eyes. I could feel it in your brain. Your thirst for the crown has meant more to you than your brood. *The gashes do better upon them.* And if you should win today – if you should win, my friend – Malcolm's back will feel the probing of your knife.

Two little boys perched on a ladder collecting eggs.
Goats cropping grass on a hillside.
An old man making a paper boat for a boy.

Another day, another village! Staring out from between the bars! Two old nags pulling a cart with a wooden cage! My hair and beard grown long! Clothes in rags and an old torn blanket against the cold! Nights getting colder as we plod the northern route! Baited with the rabble's curse! The show and gaze of the time! A rare and present monster! Painted upon a pole! The wagon creaking slowly into the courtyards! The thumping of the drum as the people assemble! The town-criers shouting to raise a crowd! Here you may see the tyrant, late deposed!

"There will be no mercy in heaven for those two."
"They will dwell in the lowest circle of the pit of hell."

One pure drop of water - afraid to offer kindness - horrible imaginings - buckling on armour - the healing agent - a ring in his nose - never for herself - need be no mystery - banners fluttering - make this journey alone.

You know, I was just a boy at the time. And my father was a thane. And the king, at that time, was old Malcolme, Duncan's father.

And my father was getting old. I was the child of a late-life birth. And it was the only time he ever talked in this way.

My father was the king's chief falconer. He organized the gamekeepers and the birds. We were testing out conditions for the king's next hunt.

"Can you tell me where I can find my two sisters?
We have very important work to do today."

Face to face with my old friend, Macduff. *Turn, hell hound turn.* You stand and stare and restore your breath. You have been in the thick of the fighting. I see nicks and cuts all over your helmet and sword. *I have avoided thee.* Blood and mud crest your armour. You have slogged in the thick today. I give you credit for your valour. Fighting courageously til the end. *Get thee back.*

You were always the weaker fighter, my friend. Always the smaller boy. *My soul is too much charged.* Sometimes you bested Banquo – sometimes not. *My voice is in my sword.* But always – at the highest level – always, always, always – your talent and your determination were never enough. *Bloodier villain.* As when we were children – as when we were youth – your efforts today will fall prey to the champion – Macbeth!

Engaging in the battle.
Crushing all my foes.

Manhandled and wrestled out of the cage! An iron ring cuts into my throat! Tugged forward on a chain to the midst of the crowd! Prodded with sharpened sticks! Spit on by women and children! Kicked and punched as I stagger along amidst the abuse! I no longer whirl and snarl as I used to do! A raised platform in the courtyard! Now the arrival of the king! Forced to listen to the taunts! All hail Malcolm! King of Scotland! Long may he reign!

A man for whom blood is a tasty elixir.
A man who gives evil creatures a ride on his back.

What is amiss - the tide rolls out - a load off weary shoulders - should accompany old age - a simple feint - lean over the parapet - surfaced again and again - try to be ghosts - two swans mating - forged in the hottest fire.

"The first time, they told me that I was too young," my father said. "The second time, they told me that I was too old." And then he held out his arm with the falcon beneath the hood.

It was a beautiful summer's day. The dogs were waiting to flush the smaller birds from the thickets. Falcons will circle above the fields and await their prey.

"I've often wondered what might have been," my father said. The falcon left his arm and began its circular climb. "Well, there are other things in life than being a king."

The lady made a prediction; the husband made a prediction.
Neither of these predictions turned out to be true.

I have waited for this moment. We are taking each other's measure. We are standing face to face. We stand bestride a kingdom like statues at Rhodes. *Thy keen sword.* I squeeze my fist on my sword. I am ready for you if you should make the first move. *Thou losest labour.* I have something I want to tell you. *Make me bleed.* It is the story of your life – and of your death. *Let fall on vulnerable crests.* I tell the stories of all the souls who live in Scotland. *I bear a charmed life.* I take their journeys and shift them onto my chosen path. *Must not yield to one of woman born.* And you – my friend – are the latest whose story I tell.

Dead bodies littering a wet and muddy battlefield.
Voices calling a name from deep in the fog.
A question of who shall wear the crown.

A crowd completely silent as the king and queen ride by.
A torturer heating an instrument in the glowing forge.
A tapestry burnt and trampled into the mud.

Who can say I bound up wounds?
Who can say I soothed the afflicted?
Who can say I shared my water; shared my food?

There is a pause in all the action. The armies cease to fight and turn our way. Boots squelch in mud and swords sag down at sides. We stand and heave our chests and suck in air. *Despair thy charm.* A grim grin spreads like a snarl across his face. *The angel whom thou servest.* His dry and cracked lips open. The sound is like thunder rolling across the sky. *Macduff was from his mother's womb untimely ripped.* He is telling me a story that splits my ears.

Relying on my predictions.
About to unseam Macduff.

Ordered to lower myself to the ground! Kneel, tyrant, kneel! My feet kicked out from under me! I roll around and raise myself up on my knees! Refusing to kiss young Malcolm's feet! A rain of blows but I will not yield! Malcolm's muddy boots upon my back! He would never have dared when his father was alive! One blow from me and he would have been choking in blood! Behold the fate of the tyrant! How my father would have rejoiced! We shall exhibit him all over Scotland! Behold my human footstool! Macbeth shall be my footstool in every town!

A man who dances with witches about a cauldron.
A man whose wife is the chief victim of his escapades.

Ambushed at the crossroads - for once and for all - dressed in gilt - look like the time - a burden to bear alone - concentrate solely on me - one single being - the right and the wrong - look for a stool - show my bloody hands.

There was a man stretched out on the rack. He had been captured and beaten and starved. And he had been laid out on the rack and his limbs had been stretched.

He had been like this for days. Perhaps a week. Every day they tightened the rack a little more.

His face was swollen and one eye was closed. Many of his bones had been snapped. The trick is that you never break the skin.

What was known became a riddle.
What was a riddle became what was known.

I will not sink under these waters. I have surfaced again and again. Every ear is tuned to hear me. Every eye is on my lips. Untimely ripped from your mother's womb, is it? *Accursed be the tongue.* A likely story to tell. *My better part of man.* I have known you since you were merely a boy and there has never been a rumour of such a deliverance. *These juggling fiends.* You sense that the witches are on my side. You have heard of their assurance concerning man of woman born. *Palter with us in a double sense.* You seek – by dissembling – to give me a counterblast. *Break it to our hope.* If witches lie, can humans not lie too?

Breakers tumbling on the edge of a kingdom.
Seagulls circling over a beach with the sun on their wings.
A man and a woman and a boy walking hand in hand.

Oh you witches! What have you done! Why would you waste a prediction on such a tiny atom as Banquo? How could such a one be hailed as the father of kings? He lacked the royal jelly! He had no sovereign prerogative in him! – not in his gestures, not in his words, not in his thoughts! He was a man who was fit to serve, but not to lead! He would surely have been content with a lesser reward! You witches have failed to complete your designated task! You cannot make your predictions by whim alone! You must be sure to take reality into account! Thoughts have consequences which you must always attempt to predict! Words inevitably lead to deeds! You should have known this all along! You must think about what you do before you act!

"They betrayed the deepest values of humanity."
"They never had a thought but for themselves."

Scorching the land - a dagger hovering - look for that meadow - completely unprepared - my deepest thoughts - should have died hereafter - present fears - you have no idea - riding through the fog - spilt milk is a problem.

And the torturers were asking him questions. What was his knowledge about Macduff? And at every denial they would give him a jolt of pain.

And I stood behind the shoulder of the master-torturer. And this man with one eye looked straight through to the back of my skull. And I knew that he had told everything he had known.

"I'm sure there's more he can tell," I said. "I'm sure he's about to crack." I clapped the torturer on the shoulder and left the cell.

They were trying to solve a riddle which was taking forever.
It was the riddle of the nature of humankind.

I stand and pant and think. He stands and pants as well. The armies pause in their fighting and crowd around us and watch as the game is played. *Yield thee, coward.* You – my friend – are an agent of these same fiends that you say you despise. Well, this steel shall test your logic. I see your words as another challenge. Know – my friend – that I have overcome challenges before. *Show and gaze of the time.* I stand before you as your king. The witches challenged me and I rose to regal size. *Our rarer monsters.* I am the only one to stand up when the witches call. *Painted upon a pole.* I understand these witches. I am one with them in mind. Banquo never saw that the witches were leading us on. Nor you – my friend – when you speak of your miracle birth. *Here you may see the tyrant.* The witches do not know the future. All of life to them is a spectacle. They set mighty forces in motion. Oppositions like you and me. Then they take a soft seat on the sidelines. They enjoy our petty struggles. They cackle and chuckle as they await the surprise at the end.

Wisdom is
the waterfall.

A host barring the door against intruders.
The heads of traitors raised on poles.
A scorpion burrowing into a skull.

Action is
the rock beneath.

"There is an old wives' tale that scorpions are able to read the minds of their victims."

Some drink their fill
while others
slip and fall.

Who can say I acted with kindness?
Petted the kitten – fed the dog?
Who can say I believe I have earned my final repose?

Time to end this exhausting spectacle. The battlefield reeks of dismembered corpses. Horses and men all stink alike as rotting flesh. The armies stand and watch the titans. Waiting to ascertain where their future loyalties will lie. *I will not yield.* My friend is breathing heavily. There is blood above his left eye. He keeps his dagger-hand too low – the fault of a novice. For such small flaws – my friend – we pay a heavy price. *I will try the last.* I see a tiny opening. Macduff's weight is on his back foot. I am exhausted but I summon up strength from deep inside. *Lay on, Macduff.* The righteous arrow always has the truest flight. I grunt and give my sword a mighty heave.

Three Books

Lord and Lady Macbeth: Full of Scorpions is My Mind – a novel

Lord and Lady Macbeth are being stung, not by scorpions, but by imagery, the medium by which human beings think at the deepest levels. And the kingdom which they seek to conquer and control is not just Scotland, but the kingdom of the mind. Imagery enlightens, but it also obscures; imagery is loyal, but it also betrays; imagery is visible on the surface, but manifests itself at hidden depths. Their mutual struggle -- to live in prose while thinking in imagery -- affects the two Macbeths in different ways.

The Making of Full of Scorpions is My Mind – a reflective journal

This journal records the author's reflections on the process of the crafting of the novel as it evolved through the stages of planning, writing, editing and polishing. It constitutes an effort to be as conscious as possible of the process whereby the single idea that suggested the topic of the novel is expanded into a complex work of art. Topics range from the nuts and bolts of novel-building to the nature of the novel as an art-form.

Planning Full of Scorpions is My Mind – a planning notebook

During the writing of the novel, the author kept a hand-written notebook which records the day-by-day development of the novel as it found its shape and style. The notebook – now in print form – reveals how a vast cluster of thoughts was sifted, selected, structured and polished into novel-form.

The Project

Together, this novel, journal and notebook comprise the twentieth installment in an on-going novel-writing project in which the author is exploring the concept of form and meaning in the novel, and of the novel as a form of expression in the 21st Century. All of the published journals and notebooks are available for free download at www.johnpassfield.ca.

About the Author

John Passfield was born in St. Thomas, Ontario, Canada, and continues to reside in Southern Ontario, near Cayuga, with his family. He has taught and studied literature, creative writing and drama, and is interested in the development of the novel as an art-form.

Novels by John Passfield

Grave Song
The Agony of Robert Chisholm

Jumbo
P. T. Barnum's Greatest Creation

Pinafore Park
The Swan Boat Incident

Water Lane
The Pilgrimage of Christopher Marlowe

Rain of Fire
The Ordeal of Conductor Spettigue

Victoria Day
The Fabric of the Community

The Wright Brothers
Flight is Possible

Leni Riefenstahl
The Valley of the Shadow

Babe Ruth
Out of the Park

Raskolnikov
Murder with an Axe

Sergei Eisenstein
Death Day

Albert Einstein
Wonder

Geoffrey Chaucer
Canterbury Bound

Ospringe
A Visit with Grandad

Pompeii
Vesuvius Dominus

Beethoven
The Ninth Immersion

Job
The Cornerstone of the Universe

Bethune
The Only Person Alive in the World

Terry Fox
Somewhere the Hurting Must Stop

Lord and Lady Macbeth
Full of Scorpions Is My Mind

Cyril Passfield
Out West

Glenn Gould
Light and Dark

See www.johnpassfield.ca for publishing information.

In Search of Form and Meaning: Journals by John Passfield

Each journal is a day-by-day record of the complex process that a writer undergoes while crafting a work of art. It records the largest decisions, of structure and theme, and the smallest decisions, such as the choice of one word over another, and the constant interaction between the two. Each journal is a record of a writer's reflection on the craft of novel-writing.

The Making of Grave Song

The Making of Jumbo

The Making of Pinafore Park

The Making of Water Lane

The Making of Rain of Fire

The Making of Victoria Day

The Making of Flight is Possible

The Making of The Valley of the Shadow

The Making of Out of the Park

The Making of Murder with an Axe

The Making of Death Day

The Making of Wonder

The Making of Canterbury Bound

The Making of Ospringe

The Making of Vesuvius Dominus

The Making of The Ninth Immersion

The Making of The Cornerstone of the Universe

The Making of The Only Person Alive in the World

The Making of Somewhere the Hurting Must Stop

The Making of Full of Scorpions Is My Mind

The Making of Out West

The Making of Glenn Gould: Light and Dark

See www.johnpassfield.ca for publishing information.

The Novel as an Art-Form:
Planning Notebooks by John Passfield

Each planning notebook is a printed version of the hand-written notebook which records the planning, writing, editing and polishing of each novel. Each notebook is an attempt to record, understand, and organize the vast cluster of thoughts which occur as one grapples with the various levels of organization which a clear yet complex work of art demands.

Planning Grave Song

Planning Jumbo

Planning Pinafore Park

Planning Water Lane

Planning Rain of Fire

Planning Victoria Day

Planning Flight is Possible

Planning The Valley of the Shadow

Planning Out of the Park

Planning Murder with an Axe

Planning Death Day

Planning Wonder

Planning Canterbury Bound

Planning Ospringe

Planning Vesuvius Dominus

Planning The Ninth Immersion

Planning The Cornerstone of the Universe

Planning The Only Person Alive in the World

Planning Somewhere the Hurting Must Stop

Planning Full of Scorpions Is My Mind

Planning Out West

Planning Glenn Gould: Light and Dark

See www.johnpassfield.ca for publishing information.

www.ingramcontent.com/pod-product-compliance
Lightning Source LLC
Chambersburg PA
CBHW030910080526
44589CB00010B/229
* 9 7 8 1 7 7 2 4 4 1 6 9 7 *